Shaped by the Master's H... ... walked the treacherous road of childhood secrets filled with ...holism, abuse, and betrayal. This book is the powerful testimony of a once-struggling Christian who ultimately discovered that she could find hope and healing not only in God's Word, but also from the hearts and minds of those who have walked that same lonely road and those who have helped them along the way.

—SHELLEY MAURICE-MAIER
Christian therapist, speaker, and author
The Sampler: Ten Life-Enhancing Concepts Right at Your Fingertips

Lolita Robinson is one of the most inspring people I have ever met. It is not only what she shares, but how she shares it that will inspire in readers a gritty hope—a hope that speaks of reality-based courage and perseverance. *Shaped by the Master's Hands* is a testimony to the power of human effort alongside the mystery of God's presence during severe trials.

—DR. KEITH M. DOUDS
Clinic Director
Meier Clinics, Long Beach, CA

For more than ten years I have watched Lolita grow emotionally and spirtually. At those times when I worked with her as her individual therapist, I was often impressed by her ability to grow through adversity. In pursing her passion and gift as a writer, Lolita now shares her story in *Shaped by the Master's Hands*. Her message will encourage anyone who is struggling to find hope in the aftermath of childhood abuse.

—CHERYL JONES-DIX, LCSW

Shaped by the Master's Hands

The Many Ways
God Mends Broken People

Lolita Robinson

ABIDING BOOKS

CONDON, OREGON

SHAPED BY THE MASTER'S HANDS
published by Abiding Books
© 2006 by Lolita Robinson
International Standard Book Number: 0-9744284-9-3

Cover design by Crown Marketing and Design
Cover image by Getty Images
Interior design and typesetting by Katherine Lloyd, The DESK

Unless otherwise indicated, Scripture quotations are from:
The Holy Bible, New International Version
© 1973, 1984 by International Bible Society,
used by permission of Zondervan Publishing House

Other Scripture quotations:
New American Standard Bible (NASB)
© 1960, 1977 by the Lockman Foundation

Printed in the United States of America

For information:
ABIDING BOOKS
P.O. BOX 243
CONDON OR 97823

Library of Congress Cataloging-in-Publication Data
Robinson, Lolita.
  Shaped by the master's hands : the many ways God mends broken people /
by Lolita Robinson.
    p. cm.
  ISBN 0-9744284-9-3 (alk. paper)
  1. Robinson, Lolita. 2. Christian biography--United States. 3. Women
musicians--United States--Biography. I. Title.
  BR1725.R6248A3 2005
  277.3'083092--dc22

                                                    2005030603

06 07 08 09 10 11 12—10 9 8 7 6 5 4 3 2 1 0

To Maurice and Clarence—
inspiration from the past

To Darrell, Joseph, Charmaine, Nikolas, and Seth—
hope for the future

Contents

PART IV: ON THE POTTER'S WHEEL

MORE THAN THANKS...

To Judith St. Pierre and Shirley Windward for using the precision and expertise of diamond cutters in preparing this manuscript. To my mother and Ari for hanging in there. We made it!

To Jim Kielty, the Crims, Diana, Arlene, Wilma Smith, Jay and Brenda Sterling, Kay Tosti, and Carole Roberts for more support than I ever could have imagined.

To my beacons of light through many dark and lonely years: Dr. Keith Douds, Gordon Broderson, Cheryl Jones-Dix, Dr. John Townsend, Dr. Henry Cloud, Dr. David Stoop, Dr. Daniel McQuoid, Monday Night Solutions, Dr. Riley, my support group, my musical family in the Jay Sterling Orchestra, Christian Life Church, and all the other brothers and sisters in my extended family, especially Cyndi C., Dorothy L., D. Robinson, and Will Miller.

To my Master, Jesus Christ, for the many ways You have used to mend a broken vessel like me.

Introduction

A MARRED VESSEL

One sunny morning in the fall of 1986, my mother and I went shopping at Robinsons-May in West Los Angeles. I had an interview scheduled with a major gospel recording company in two days, and Mom was buying me a new outfit. She and I laughed and chatted like two schoolgirls, rejoicing in my opportunity to jump-start the singing career I had always wanted but had walked away from in my twenties.

A few months earlier, I had run into an old acquaintance from show business. I told him that I wanted to get back into singing and asked if he had any contacts. He gave me the telephone number of the artist relations representative at a major gospel label. When I phoned her, she said, "I don't have a lot of time, but come on in." Now I was flitting around the store, trying to find just the right outfit for my meeting. I finally settled on a tan pantsuit with a beige hat, a cream-colored sash to match, and taupe high heels.

I knew that my chances in the secular music industry

were nil because at thirty-one, I was too old. But I dared to hope the Lord would open the door for me to sing gospel, even though I'd never had any desire to sing Christian music before. My thinking at the time was, *Well, if it's too late for a big secular career, I might as well try my luck in the gospel field.* I had no idea there was any difference between entertainment and ministry. I thought the two were the same.

It had been years since I'd recorded anything, but I wasn't entirely unprepared. I had sung secular music professionally for more than fifteen years before I put the brakes on my career, and when I unexpectedly received a small inheritance, I used some of it to work with Marcel East, a talented producer. I had a professional tape made, and with that, my glowing résumé, a few newspaper clippings of reviews, some pictures, and a showstopping outfit, I felt confident about my upcoming interview. I really thought I had my act together.

On the day of the big meeting, I sat in my car trying to get up the nerve to go inside the recording company. Turning the radio to the classical station, I rolled down the window and let the cool breeze wash over me. I closed my eyes and prayed. Moments later, feeling refreshed, I walked through the front door of the tall glass building.

As soon as I stepped off the elevator into the office, my legs began to shake. I immediately saw that I was way overdressed. The young employees were clad casually in jeans and sweaters. Wearing that hat, I must have looked like Sally Field in *The Flying Nun.* I was terrified that all eyes were on me, and I wanted to cry.

The receptionist at the front desk greeted me in a friendly manner, but there was a strong smell of professionalism in the air. I told her I was there to see Sara. By then I wanted to sneak out and run. It was one thing to dream about taking my singing tape to a major label, but actually doing so was a real wake-up call. Taking the first available seat in the lobby, I waited to be called. I tried desperately to steady my hands on my lap. They were shaking so badly that I could hardly hold on to my media kit.

While I was checking out the competition, I watched the young man and two women seated near me. They sat back, confidently thumbing through magazines. All three appeared calm and assured. *Well,* I figured, w*hen in Rome, do as the Romans do,* and I grabbed a magazine from the top of the stack. It was filled with technical black and white pictures of the latest computers. It was totally boring, but I wasn't about to put it back and risk someone seeing my shaking hands, so I read it. It worked. The magazine was so mind-numbingly dull that it settled my nerves. I sat back and crossed my legs, dangling one foot like the others, pretending to be cool. But inside I was a wreck. I felt like a four-year-old playing copycat.

Then came the big moment. The fresh-faced receptionist called my name. "Sara will see you now," she said, pointing in the direction I was to go. I walked down the hall, took a deep breath, and knocked on Sara's door.

When I stepped into the room, a tall woman stood up from behind her desk and graciously shook my hand. The formalities over, I handed her my material. I sat very still as she pored over the information in the packet. When she plopped my tape into the recorder, my heart was beating so fast I could hardly breathe. After listening to the first song, she called to one of her colleagues in the next office. A young man who looked like a college student came into the room. Sara flashed me a radiant smile. "I like what I'm hearing," she said. "This is very good."

My heart soared. I wanted to leap out of my seat, run behind the desk, and squeeze her tight. Instead, I just thanked her profusely. The guy was bobbing his head to the beat of the music. "Cool," he said as he left the room.

Sara told me she would be gone on company business for six weeks. As soon as she returned, she would contact me to discuss the next steps. I shook her hand joyfully, hightailed it past the receptionist's desk, and made a beeline to my car, tearfully praising the Lord. When I got home, I called my mother. "They liked me!" I shrieked. "They liked me!" We screamed and cheered in celebration.

14

At the time, I had been working for six years as a receptionist for a manufacturing company. I enjoyed my job and loved my coworkers, but I still wanted to sing. When I returned to work that day, no one knew why I was practically doing pirouettes up and down the hallways. My colleagues stared at me, wondering what was going on, but I didn't tell anyone I had hit the jackpot. Something told me to wait until the plans were finalized before I spoke up. Secretly, though, I made plans for my swan song. I planned to give my two-week notice after Sara called me back, and I envisioned sitting at the conference table one morning telling the crew that I would be leaving soon to make my debut album.

Thank God I put a sock in my mouth.

Six weeks came and went with no word. I called the record company and left message after message, but I got no response. I was furious. Even if they weren't interested, they could have had the courtesy to call to say, "Thanks, but we've changed our minds." I would have expected that kind of treatment from a secular record company, but I naively expected something different from a Christian label. How could those who claimed to be servants of our Lord and Savior, Jesus Christ, be so indifferent toward a sister's feelings? How could they leave me hanging in limbo like that?

I never heard a word from that company. Two years later, I found out through other sources that major changes had gone down in that label and that new people had taken over. I don't know whether or not that had any bearing on my situation, but by that time it really didn't matter what the company's reasons were for not contacting me. By then I knew that God Himself had closed that door.

One rainy afternoon, after months of waiting for a call, I crept to my car during my lunch break. My heart was aching deep in my chest, and I cried and prayed. *How come I got so far, only to have the door slammed in my face?* Halfheartedly, I opened my Bible and read some passages at random. I wasn't looking for anything in particular. In fact, I was so discouraged and upset with the Lord that the last thing I expected from Him was comfort. As I turned the pages toward Proverbs, my eyes scanned other books, and a passage in Jeremiah jumped off the page and grabbed my heart:

This is the word that came to Jeremiah from the LORD. "Go down to the potter's house, and there I will give you my message." So I went down to the potter's house, and I saw him working at the wheel. But the pot he was shaping from the clay was marred in his hands; so the potter formed it into another pot; shaping it as seemed best to him. (18:1–4)

When I read those words, I understood what the Lord was saying to me. I was like a battered ship lost in a fierce storm, and that passage of Scripture turned out to be a lighthouse.

Later on that night at home, I read the Scripture again. The word *marred* stood out, and I looked it up in the dictionary. It means blemished, flawed, or damaged. I knew it described me, but I wasn't offended by it. I knew that God wasn't telling me that I was despicable in His sight or that I was damaged beyond repair or that He couldn't use me. He was showing me the condition of my soul and revealing to me the extent of my emotional injuries. I felt Him reassuring me that He was going to restore me and do a new work in my life.

"'Can I not do with you as this potter does?' declares the LORD. 'Like clay in the hand of the potter, so are you in my hand'" (v. 6). In tears, I lowered my head in prayer: *I will allow You to mold me as You see fit, Father.* At that moment, I knew that I was in the Master's hands and that He was beginning to shape me into a worthy vessel. What I did not know was what a long and painful process my restoration would be. Nor did I realize how many different ways God uses to mend broken vessels like me.

PART I

A Flawed Mold

MIRACLE IN LOMPOC

SHIRLEY WINDWARD

That autumn, bulldozers came
grumping over the field of flowers outside
our window, plowing through our view.

Then the rakers ambled in
turning all they touched to curried loam
and the tar-fellows followed with creaking
noxious carts, spreading black death
over the earth. They took a long while;
we took to shutting our doors.

By the time winter enfolded us,
wanton gravel trucks, like great dogs,
at the water hydrant, arrived to spray a six-inch
layer of little stones—and then someone
in charge laid down over the ravaged field
a thick final splash of macadam, scoring it
with glaring white lines. The ultimate
chain fence grew overnight, and finally
we were allowed to park in the civilized way.

Spring, though somewhat
bewildered, stepped in with grace, bringing days
of sunlight, pricking our faces in
small showers; and at last an hour came
when we all crowded around a great
volcanic crack parting the new black
pavement, its edges folding upward,
spearing tires as they tried to pass.

Everyone stared.

From the apex of the four-wedging crack,
from the deeper loam below the tar and gravel
one bi-leafed, exquisite shaft of green
thrust up to greet us
with a crimson tulip bud
tipped toward the sun.

Chapter One

A BITTERSWEET BEGINNING

*I*f you had visited my Chicago neighborhood back in the late fifties, you wouldn't have seen anything out of the ordinary. Westchester Field was an upper scale residential area—a thriving black community of hardworking people. Children's laughter filled the air as they played kickball and hopscotch, jumped rope, and pulled red wagons full of scruffy little passengers.

Doubtless, Mrs. Dutton would have been standing on her front porch dressed in her usual floral housedress, white ankle socks, and black shoes, wagging her finger and scolding. "You kids better knock it off, or I'm telling your folks." She had good reason. Those were the glorious afternoons when we woke up napping toddlers while we played tag or took great shortcuts to the park—hopping neighbors' fences, trampling their freshly mowed lawns, and crushing their flowers.

Families on our block looked out for one another. Adults

had the authority to lay down the law, and we youngsters were obliged to listen. I, for one, was chastised for running up and down the wooden stairs on the back porch and for picking lilies out of Mrs. Harris's garden. We little darlings stole fruit from trees and rode other children's bikes without permission. Some—I won't say who—even snatched candy and gum from the corner drugstore.

In the frosty winter months we bundled up in snow pants, mittens, scarves, boots, and Martian-looking pointed woolen caps with a red, yellow, or blue ball dangling from the top. When summer rolled around again, we chucked our body armor and took to the streets like soldiers escaping from a prison camp.

Block parties were the first sign of the glorious start of summer vacation. The neighbors would block off the entrances at both ends of the street, and I would dash from house to house borrowing whatever my family needed to make our contribution to the potluck. The outdoors smelled of backyard barbecues—juicy hot dogs, greasy ribs, half-burned burgers, and succulent chicken. Tables along the street groaned under the weight of freshly baked fruit pies and cakes, fruit salads, watermelon, and corn on the cob. Some people sat on their front porches churning homemade vanilla ice cream.

I never knew how, but someone figured out a way to play music from stereos so it could be heard up and down the street. I walked around giggling, watching the ones I loved popping their fingers and swaying their hips to the beat of the latest record craze. We listened to Fats Domino, Johnny Mathis, and Nat King Cole, but it was the toe-tapping rhythm of Ray

Charles's music that sent me swooning. Pretty soon people really relaxed, and just as Motown later sang about, there was dancing in the streets.

After we kids had eaten enough to batter even the strongest stomach, we would trot off to Tulley or Abbott Park to play in the sprinklers. Some afternoons, the firemen from the local fire station down the street would yell to us, "Come on, kids, we're turning on the fire hydrants!" Off we'd run fully clothed for the soaking of a lifetime.

My frolics with the neighborhood children gave me sense of belonging that I otherwise lacked. On our block, I was the only child of a single mother. Everyone else I knew came from an intact home with a mother, father, and siblings. I wondered all the time why my life was so different. My mother and I seemed to live in our own separate corner of the world, and it was painful to feel that something was wrong with us because she had no husband and I had no father.

Kids often asked me, "Where's your dad?" My stomach would churn and my thoughts would race as I tried to come up with an answer. But I never had any, so I'd finally say, "I don't know."

I never asked my mother about my father, but once when I asked my grandmother where he was, she told me that he had been killed while serving in the air force.

Why did he go and leave my mom and me behind? I asked myself.

My mother and I shared an upstairs bedroom in my grandparents' three-story, four-bedroom house. Our bedroom was wedged in between my grandmother and grandfather's bedrooms, and the sun didn't shine in there because the house next door obstructed the light. The room was gloomy, and even when I was very young, I didn't like to stay in there any longer than necessary.

It was the same bedroom my mother had occupied before I was born, although it didn't look like a teenager's room. There were no posters of faraway places, school memorabilia, or pictures of America's latest heartthrob plastered on the walls and no stuffed animals or records strewn on the floor. There were no fancy clothes or shoes in the closet, no vanity with a mirror and makeup, no colorful bottles of nail polish or fruity, sweet-smelling perfumes. The brown, dreary room had a double bed that we shared and an old brown dresser that took up most of the space and blocked the closet door.

I used to lie in the bed next to my mother early in the morning and braid her hair. I'd stare in her face, thinking how pretty she was. My earliest memories of her are a study in stark contrasts. I have pleasant memories of her hugging and kissing me and showering me with many gifts. Whatever my mother lacked in pretty things, she made sure that I had bright, frilly clothes and toys. Yet she wasn't around much, and when she was, she was often distant. She was an elusive shadow who seemed to float in and out of my existence, like a fairy princess bearing gifts when she arrived.

Perhaps my mother's room was a reflection of her inner suffering. I don't think she was ever a carefree, happy child. Did my grandparents see her pain? Or did she hide it as she did her pregnancy? Wearing a coat in the month of June should have signaled that something was terribly wrong, but no one who knew the truth seemed to know how to help her. At seventeen, my mother bore the brunt of responsibility for what had transpired between her and the man who had sexually molested and then seduced her. Only a handful of her friends stood by her, realizing that she was a victim and a child herself when she gave birth to me.

My birth was not a celebrated event. It was a heavy shadow that hovered over our family for many years to come. I now see the dark, oppressive room that my mother and I shared as a metaphor for the emotional devastation that would ravage both our lives.

My grandparents, the Maxwells, were admired and respected in our community, and I loved them dearly. They weren't your traditional couple. The balance of power was evenly distributed in their relationship. They shared the decision making, and both provided financially for the family. Grandfather worked for General Mills for more than thirty years. Grandmother graduated with a master's degree and became one of the first black female parole officers in Illinois, a huge accomplishment in the forties. They had six children, three boys and three girls. My mom was the youngest. Their eldest son was killed in a stabbing accident before I was born. I was told that he and a friend had been playing a game of chicken with knives.

Saturday mornings were special times in my grandparents' home. With her hair pulled back into a stylish French twist and an apron covering her housedress, Grandmother would whip up a spectacular breakfast for the entire family. The smell of hot coffee brewing and sausages, bacon, and ham frying filled the air. I'd run downstairs and plop down at the kitchen table, my mouth watering as I watched my grandmother pour flour and thick buttermilk into a large yellow glass bowl to make her masterpiece pancakes.

I could hardly wait for my aunts and uncles and cousins to arrive because that's when the fun began. Grandfather wasn't one for talking, but that never stopped his boisterous clan from clowning around in the kitchen. My mother and her siblings ribbed one another so much that it was like being at a comedy club.

I'd ask my grandmother a thousand times, "When are they coming?"

Her eyes sparkling behind her wire-rimmed glasses, she'd smile and say, "Hold your horses; they'll be here."

I was distraught when my cousins had to go home for they were the closest thing to siblings I had. I was the only child in that big house, and knowing they would all be back the following Saturday was the only thing that sustained me during the lonely week that followed.

On holidays and special occasions, the grown-ups entertained themselves by playing cards and dominoes or dancing to the stereo upstairs while we kids played and laughed downstairs in the family room in one of my aunts' or uncles' basements. To keep ourselves occupied, we used to have singing contests. I'd grab a record and put it on, pick up a pencil or hairbrush to use as a microphone, and then lip-synch one of my favorites, like "One Fine Day" or "You'll Never Get to Heaven."

Every once in a while we'd hear someone upstairs say,

"Man, you gonna lay your cards down—or talk all night?" I'd sneak upstairs from time to time and walk quietly from room to room trying to get close to the adults. On every table were beer cans or clear glasses filled with ice cubes and hard liquor. Our clan was known for throwing a good party, and drinking was a normal activity at all our gatherings.

Those parties were both sweet and bitter, like the large picture of a clown one of my aunts had hung downstairs in her family room. The clown wore the traditional white, red, and black makeup, but he looked miserable. He was holding a flower, but his jowls sagged, and his expression was full of despair. His mouth turned downward, and he stared straight ahead with his large, round coal-black eyes. I would stare into the eyes of that unhappy clown, feeling empty and lonely as I listened to the music and the laughter upstairs. That picture reminded me of my family, and it scared me. Underneath our happy exterior, dark secrets plagued us all.

Another family that touched my life profoundly and shaped my future was an elderly, childless couple who had known our family since my mother was a little girl. When I was three months old, Mama Hall agreed to take care of me while my mother was at work. In her absence, the Halls became my parents, and while I was in their care, there were long periods of time when I wasn't quite sure I'd ever see my mother again.

Mama Hall reminded me of the great black actress Bea Richards. She had a dark complexion, hauntingly expressive eyes, and an air of sadness about her. Every morning she and I listened to Southern black gospel music on the radio as she did her ironing and other chores. The adults in the Maxwell family sent my cousins and me to church, but they didn't attend with us, and my first impression of religion was that believing in God was optional and that however you chose to serve Him was fine. But at the Halls, we attended church faithfully as a family. When I was two, I started singing in church. I'd come home and teach my cousins the songs I'd learned in Sunday school.

The Halls weren't rich, but they were comfortable, and between them and my mother, I never lacked anything. While the Halls indulged me, they also taught me the value of hard work and the meaning of gratitude. I was never under the illusion that life owed me anything. I saw hard work and perseverance demonstrated in different ways in both my grandparents' and the Halls' homes.

However, the Halls provided me with more order, predictability, and stability, and that gave me the sense of safety I lacked at home, where the older cousins, not the adults, looked out for the younger ones. Parental supervision was lax; boundaries were blurred. Not so with the Halls. Mama ran a tight ship. She set schedules for me to follow, assigned me chores to do, and saw to it that I bathed and went to bed at a regular time. Whenever Dad Hall was home, we sat at the table and ate meals together as a family. There was no partying or alcohol in their house.

Mama Hall took great pride in keeping an impeccably neat home. In fact, everyone joked that her house was so clean you could eat off the floors. You could bounce a quarter off a bed she made, just like they do in those old army movies. She covered all the furniture in clear plastic coverings and would wash and iron new clothes just brought from the store. My diapers, they told me, were white and freshly pressed before she dressed me. Nothing was ever out of order in Mama Hall's home, and she was very proud of the fact that she had taught me from an early age never to touch anything in the house without permission. She often told people, "Lolita was a good baby; she never bothered anything that didn't belong to her."

Back then I was proud that I was a good little girl. I learned early to conduct myself like a little adult, and I tried very hard to stay out of people's way. But I was also lonely.

Mama Hall didn't want other children to come inside and mess up the place, so I had to think of ways to keep myself entertained. Sometimes I'd watch game shows and soap operas on television while Mama sewed and did her ironing. But they were so boring that even now I get depressed at the thought of watching daytime dramas. Mama had miniature decorative figurines of animals and little girls spread through-out the house, and sometimes I'd imagine I was one of those glass ceramic decorations and wonder what its life was like. Or I'd go play in the Halls' back bedroom. I would stand in front of the big vanity mirror on Mama Hall's mahogany dresser and perform songs I made up to pretend audiences. When I finished singing, I'd take my bows.

I knew that Mama loved me. At times she would hold me close, hugging and kissing me and letting me know that I was her heart. But there were also times when she accused me of being lazy because my cleaning abilities paled in comparison to hers. Sometimes she would complain about my appearance. While combing my hair, she often told me I looked like a sage hen. I took her comments to heart.

During the summer months, Mama let me sit in Dad's favorite red easy chair and wait up for him. She would sit in her chair braiding her thinning hair into little braids all over her head while we watched Jack Parr or Johnny Carson. Those were special times between Mama and me. In the evenings she was more relaxed and open for conversation. During those quiet moments, I sometimes tried to fish for information about my family.

"Mama, did you ever know my real dad in the air force?"

Her expression wouldn't change as she stared at the television. Her answer was always the same: "No, baby, I didn't." Then she would change the subject.

And sometimes when I asked to go play outside, she would say, "You're just like your mother and her gang. All you want to do is rip and run the streets." Her remarks pierced my heart. I had no idea what she meant by *running the streets,* but it didn't sound good.

I loved both the Maxwells and the Halls, but I felt torn between the two families, and trying to adjust to so many different personalities made life very confusing. Mama Hall complained that my mother and her siblings were irresponsible. She had great respect for my grandparents, but not for their child rearing. For their part, some members of the Maxwell family laughed at my church songs and said hurtful things about Mama Hall. They called her a religious nut and an old gossip. When the two families behaved that way toward each other, they sent me mixed messages, and I felt insecure and somehow responsible for their feelings.

Chapter Two

ROOTS OF INSECURITY

Grandfather Maxwell was a quiet man with a daily ritual. He got up at dawn, dressed, and walked up the street to the corner market to buy a newspaper. When he got back home, he fed his dog Smokey and then sipped a cup of coffee and smoked a Chesterfield cigarette while he read the paper. After that he went to work at General Mills. He wasn't big on displaying affection, but he opened a savings account at Pullman Bank for each one of his grandchildren and faithfully deposited money in our accounts. That was his way of showing us how he felt.

I loved my grandfather and enjoyed his company, but he puzzled me. There seemed to be two grandfathers inside him. There was the quiet, reserved, hardworking man who spent long hours in the backyard tending to my grandmother's yellow roses and sitting quietly with me watching baseball games or the evening news. Other times, there was a loud, gregarious fellow who cracked jokes, but smelled funny.

Grandfather had Indian ancestry, and when he became talkative, he would sit us kids down and tell us stories about his Blackfoot family. He said his Indian name was "Sada." We kids were elated that Sada wanted to spend so much time with us. We were allowed to ask him any question we could think of, and he'd answer it. He would laugh and beckon for Grandmother to sit next to him. "Come on over here and sit down, gal," he'd say, but she'd ignore him and look perturbed. I watched the expression on my grandmother's face and on the faces of the rest of the family when Grandfather was in that state. They were stoic and detached. Why didn't they think he was funny? How come they weren't laughing at his marvelous tales? "Not now, Daddy," one of my aunts or uncle would say.

What I couldn't have known was that for years my grandfather had tormented his wife and children during violent, alcoholic outbursts. By the time I was born, he had mellowed into what you would call a binge drinker. He'd go for months at a time without a drop of alcohol, but then drink for weeks. The cycle would end when he got sick.

When that happened, I'd sit sadly in the corner. I'd hear him moaning, "I'm sorry; I'm sorry," while he vomited up blood. Without any warning, the outgoing, talkative, funny grandfather would disappear, and the distant, withdrawn man would reappear. It was a sad and confusing transition for my young mind, but I always felt protective of him. For some reason, I understood him.

Dad Hall was a reserved man with a gentle nature. He was the breadwinner and decision maker in the home. A diligent, hardworking man, he worked at the steel mill and owned a local dry-cleaning business. Along with holding down two jobs, he did all the maintenance and repairs around the Halls' small home. He kept his yard as faithfully as any groundskeeper at a luxurious hotel.

Dad Hall was the only man in my life who ever gave me a sense of being "Daddy's little girl." I felt loved, adored, and cherished whenever he was around. He had a red van that he used to pick up and deliver clothing to patrons of his cleaners, and some days I went with him when he made deliveries. We'd stop and visit other businesses or personal friends. They'd always greet me with a tender "Hey, little miss." Dad smiled proudly as his friends teased me.

On the evenings Dad came home late, Mama would prepare him a snack. He loved crackers and cheese heated up in an aluminum pie pan. Then Dad and I had our special time together in the kitchen. He'd fix himself a cup of coffee and pour some in a white cup for me, drowning mine in milk. Dangling my legs beneath my big chair, I would sip my coffee and chat like a little lady.

"Daddy, are you going to tickle me?" I'd ask him, squealing with delight.

He'd sit still and say with a straight face, "Me? Would I do something like that?" He'd look at me out the corner of his eye, pause for a second, then smile and gently grab me and tickle my sides.

We'd laugh until Mama called out: "Quiet down in there, you two. It's getting late, and it's time for someone we know to go to bed."

Dad would put his finger to his lips and whisper, "Shhh! See what you made me do?"

We'd snicker and giggle more quietly so Mama wouldn't put me to bed.

I often wondered why Mama was never a part of our fun times. She'd fix Dad's snack and then go back into the living room and finish watching her program. I just figured Johnny Carson was captivating; it never dawned on me that she was never invited to join us. Dad Hall was kind and loving to me, but he was very distant from Mama.

Unfortunately, the special times I spent with Dad Hall were fleeting moments because he was hardly ever home. It turned out that his personality was as complex as my grandfather's. There were two Dad Halls, just as there were two grandfathers, although for different reasons. Mama told me repeatedly that Dad Hall worked long hours to provide for us, but years later I discovered there was much more to the story: Dad Hall was seeing other women.

When I was a child, nothing in my life was as it appeared.

The most important men in the first few years of my life were confusing to me. Opposing aspects of their lives intertwined, contradictory behaviors working simultaneously, and they hid their brokenness behind masks. This was true not only of my grandfather and Dad Hall, but also of my uncle, who began to sexually molest me when I was five years old.

Uncle Hansen was married to my mother's oldest sister. When other kids weren't around, he would follow me. He pretended to be kind, and I thought he loved me because I was his niece.

I trusted him and wanted him to love me as he did his own children. My grandfather was not an affectionate man in terms of hugs and cuddling. Mr. Hall hugged, but not enough. I was starving for male attention and affection.

My grandfather and Dad Hall were bleak examples of healthy, strong, and loving men, but whatever their character defects, neither ever put a hand on me or did anything to compromise my innocence. Uncle Hansen, on the other hand, was hideous. He wooed me under the guise of caring, all the while setting a trap for me. His kindness, gifts, and avowals of love were nothing more than bait for a fish.

I spent a lot of time with the Hansen family. One of their sons, Chief, was a year older than me, and we were very close. I felt like a part of the family with my aunt and her children, but stalked by her husband. I tried my best to stay clear of him, but he was always lurking somewhere in the shadows. I cringed when he lured me into his bedroom by asking me to help him find his slippers or telling me he had a present for me. When he closed the door behind us, I shook in fear. When he touched my body, I distanced myself by studying the wallpaper or looking at the pictures on the wall. I emotionally left my body. I was too young to know how to cry out for help or even that I had the right to.

There were times at my grandparents' when others would point their fingers and whisper when I came in the room. As soon as I got close, the whispering would stop. I pretended not to notice, but I did. I thought they were whispering about me—the dirty little girl. I felt ashamed and disgusted with myself, and I saw the whispering as evidence that the whole world knew I was doing bad things. Dad Hall had painted my name on the front of his red van. He said he wanted the world to know that I was his daughter and how much he loved me. But when I saw my name written there, I felt exposed. I didn't want the neighbors to see it for fear they would discover the sick, secret games my uncle was forcing me to play.

How deceptive and crazy making the molestation was for me! Later on in life, I didn't know how to separate love from abuse. To me the two were intertwined, and in my choices of significant others they ended up being the same.

A tragic event happened on my first day of kindergarten. My best friend, Bernie, lived across the street, and his mother drove us to school. As we got close to the school yard, all of a sudden we hit a bump and the car stopped. Bernie's mother started crying and screaming hysterically. I froze. Bernie tried to open the door, but his mother screamed, "Don't touch that door. Stay put, please!"

People ran to the car, covering their mouths in horror. Bewildered, I stared straight ahead. The police arrived and tried to console my distraught neighbor. As she spoke to the officer, I stuck my head out the window and took a peek. I saw a puddle of thick, dark, reddish purple stuff by the front tire. I didn't know what it was, but from my neighbor's reaction, I knew it wasn't good. I sat back next to Bernie, perplexed. A few bystanders were crying. Eventually, one of the officers took Bernie and me away from the scene. As we left, I heard someone say, "Look, there's blood in the street. A little boy ran out in front of that car."

I could hardly wait to tell my mother what had happened. I wanted to be the first one to bring her the news. Others were always around because we lived with my grandparents, and I competed for her attention. I wanted a special bond of connection with her, even if it came in the form of telling her about a tragedy. I bolted into our house and ran to her.

My mother was sitting in the living room watching television, and when I told her about the accident, she calmly sat me on her lap. She held me, but I don't remember what she said to me. Like so many other memories of my early interactions with her, my recollection of this one is vague. I don't recall any comforting and tender words. The episode was never mentioned again, at least not to me. I did wonder later why my mother didn't take me to school my first day. Perhaps she felt more like my sister than a mother. How emotionally connected could she have been?

Her father drowned his sorrow in alcohol and was in no condition to meet the emotional needs of his daughters. Her mother escaped the stress of raising five children with an emotionally absent and sometimes violent husband by plunging headlong into pursuing a college degree. When she was growing up, my mother was basically left to fend for herself emotionally, while older siblings took up the slack for her physical care. The lack of parental involvement in my mother's daily care made her a perfect target for destruction. When she was thirteen, my father entered her life. Not long afterward, he began seducing her.

Even as a child, I saw my mother's fragility and sensed her sorrow. I wanted to make life easier on her and others, and I learned to put their feelings and welfare above my own. I got acceptance and approval by being a peacemaker and by not making waves. It never dawned on me to tell my mother that I was being sexually abused. I never shared any of my pain. I was learning to cope the way the rest of my family did, and that meant not speaking candidly about painful realities. No one ever told me not to talk; I just knew that certain subjects were taboo.

There were no heart-to-heart talks to anchor my soul. I felt like a ghost. I walked and talked and interacted with those around me, but it seemed I made no lasting impression anywhere. It was as though people could walk right through me or sit where I sat and never know the territory was occupied. I concluded that if the painful events going on around me weren't important enough to discuss, I must not be important either.

I even had doubts that I belonged to my mother. Two older members of my extended family looked more like her than I did, and they both spent a lot of time with her. I was jealous because people often mistook them for her daughters. In those days, the lighter you were, the better. The texture of your hair mattered, too. My mother was beautiful, with a light complexion and fine hair. I was darker complected with thick, coarse hair. Though society made skin color an issue, my family never did. No one told me that I looked different or had bad hair. I just looked in the mirror, and when I saw that I didn't look like my mother, I decided I was ugly and didn't fit in.

I felt threatened and insecure about my place in my mother's heart, and my school experiences didn't help my faltering self-image. I went to a public school for kindergarten, but in first and second grade I attended a parochial school.

Going to that school seemed more like attending a funeral. I couldn't figure out why people who claimed to love God and to be His servants were so miserable and mean. My first-grade teacher regularly cracked our knuckles with her pointer, even for making mistakes on our schoolwork. Once she hit me because I cut the head off of one of my art projects. The other children laughed at my headless wonder. It didn't matter to the teacher that I didn't know how to use scissors. She just said, "You just weren't following directions."

Her response confused me. I thought school was a place to learn, not to be penalized for not knowing. I withdrew in class, and to this day I'm not particularly fond of arts and crafts. That early experience made me self-conscious about making mistakes and asking for help. I didn't want to be embarrassed again, so I didn't ask for help from teachers—or from anyone else for that matter.

I had another humiliating experience in that particular class. I told my teacher that I wasn't feeling well, but she didn't listen, and I threw up in my lap. She made me get up and stand outside the door in the hallway until my family was notified. I stood holding my dress up because I didn't want the vomit to fall on the floor. When other teachers walked by, I cried and turned my head away in shame. None of them offered to help me. Eventually, someone got my seven-year-old cousin Chief out of class, and he walked me back to his house.

I never confused God with those teachers, who supposedly represented Him. I never believed that He was cold, distant, and unkind. In fact, back then I used to talk to Him all the time. I used to walk down the street and ask Him, "If You

37

took only one step, would You be in China?" Or I'd say, "God, all You have to do is wave Your hand and food will appear." I knew He was all-powerful. I loved the song "He's Got the Whole World in His Hands." I used to open my hands wide and try to figure out how God fit us all in His. One day while playing in the school yard, I told Him, "I'm not what these people call themselves. I'm a Christian, and I'm never going to be like them."

I have no idea where that revelation came from. I was only a first-grader, but the word *Christian* meant something special to me even then, and I didn't want to associate myself with my school or its denomination. Looking back, I believe the Lord had His hand on my heart, even though it would be years before I met Him personally. As young as I was, there was already a special place in my heart for God.

Second grade was a refreshing change from the previous year. My teacher was a sweet woman, and she helped me realize that a few people didn't represent everyone in a particular faith. The morbid, joyless individuals I had encountered weren't the poster children for their faith, and throughout my life I have met wonderful, loving people of that denomination.

Unfortunately, the negative experiences at school didn't help my fragile self-esteem, and I was a timid, insecure child, totally lacking the emotional resiliency I needed to face the enormous changes that were about to take place in my life.

Chapter Three

A WORLD TURNED UPSIDE DOWN

I heard footsteps stomping up the stairs and little voices whispering and snickering outside the bathroom door. Someone knocked. "Hurry up, Lolita. We got something to tell ya."

"What?" I yelled back.

"Just come on! We'll tell ya when ya get out."

I got quiet. I didn't know why, but I felt anxious. A few minutes later, I timidly opened the door. Four of my cousins stood there staring at me like hoot owls.

"What's the matter with you all?" I asked. At first no one said a word. Then Chief broke the silence. "Grandmother and them are having company downstairs," he said.

Well, I already knew that, but his next statement threw me for a curve. "Everyone came to meet your mother's new boyfriend."

SHAPED BY THE MASTER'S HANDS

My eyes widened in disbelief. *Boyfriend? I didn't know my mother had a boyfriend!*

"And he's a white, too!"

My heart started racing. "A white man?" I repeated. Their heads bobbed up and down in sync.

"What does he look like?" I asked.

Somebody said, "He's an o-o-o-ld man. He's wearing glasses."

"An old white man?" My eyes widened; I couldn't believe what I was hearing. Why on earth was my mother dating an old white man?

"Oh brother," I said. Shaking my head, I following the bearers of bad news downstairs.

People were scattered throughout the house. The music was blaring, and everyone was laughing and eating. I saw my mother over in the corner talking to a stranger. When I entered the room, all eyes turned on me. I cased the joint, looking for an old man, but I didn't see one. The nice-looking guy mother was talking to had on glasses, and he was definitely white. But he wasn't old.

My mother called to me. "Come here, baby, and meet my friend. His name is Ari."

I didn't know what to make of the situation. My mother generally didn't bring men around me. For a while she had dated a guy who had a daughter younger than me, but I never had much interaction with him. I couldn't help noticing that she looked really happy with her new friend.

Ari extended his hand and smiled. I shook his hand and looked down. When he said hello, I noticed that he had a funny accent. I spoke to him, but I kept my distance. At that moment I felt all alone and wished I had a brother or sister to help me process what was going on. My cousins were standing there, but they couldn't relate to how I felt. Their mother wasn't going out with a new white guy.

My family was multicultural, but except for some of my teachers and the local firemen, I had never had any close association with white people. Our section of town was black. The white community lived on the other side of the train tracks. We never bothered them, and they left us alone. Our family warned us never to venture across the tracks. I used to stare under the viaduct, wondering what the white people were doing, but that was the extent of my curiosity. I wasn't as concerned about Ari's skin color as I was about what role he'd play in our lives. I didn't like or dislike him; I felt numb.

Ari began coming around more and more. The Maxwells were crazy about him, and my grandmother talked about him incessantly. Both of my grandparents liked the fact that he had a good head on his shoulders. The old man my cousins had told me about was twenty-one and an exchange student at the University of Chicago. The entire family took Ari into their hearts and he them.

Ari tried to make friends with me. When he came to my seventh birthday party, he brought me a wonderful gift, "Kissy," a popular doll I really wanted. He was so proud when he handed her to me. Inside I was pleased, but I didn't show it. I took the doll quietly and went about my business. Kissie was big and cuddly, and she became my best friend, but I didn't let Ari know how special she was to me.

41

Unfortunately, Ari was too young and inexperienced to understand that I was threatened because my mother cared for him, and he took my distance personally. He had no way of knowing how fragile I was. If men I *knew* would abuse me, what would a stranger do to me? Abuse had destroyed my ability to bond and form normal attachments, and my walls and defenses were in place. I never let Ari in emotionally, and our relationship never had a chance. I wasn't going to let him, or anyone else for that matter, get close to me. His skin color had nothing to with it. I would have rejected a black man, too. The bottom line was that I didn't want any man in my mother's life.

No one told me how serious things were getting between my mother and Ari. One day Ari appeared at a dinner party; the next thing I knew they were getting married. The Halls never discussed the changes going on in my mother's life, either. Everything just unfolded. I guess everyone thought that since I was a child, there was no need to discuss anything with me. No one asked me how I felt or helped me through the transition.

I don't remember my mother's wedding day. I don't remember who was in it, what she wore, what Ari wore, or what I wore. I don't remember the guests. There was a celebration at my grandparents' home, but I don't know if the ceremony was performed there, or if they just had a reception. I do remember walking aimlessly through our dining room, looking at all the wedding gifts. I felt like a spectator watching the event.

Not long after the wedding, my grandmother started talking to me about more changes. "Isn't it great?" she said. "You've got a new dad now. Your parents will be gone for a while. They went to find you guys a new home."

I heard what my grandmother said, but I really didn't understand. I didn't know that my mother and Ari had gone three thousand miles away and would be gone close to a month. I didn't know that having a new father would mean leaving everyone I had ever loved and the only place I had ever known as home.

One day I was sitting at the sewing counter in Dad Hall's cleaners. He had one employee, a seamstress named Dot. There was something different about that day. I could tell something was wrong. Dot seemed somber as she sat on her stool sewing a hem on my doll's dress. Dad Hall was unusually quiet and barely spoke the entire morning. I watched him lay a garment on the presser, lower the heavy lid, and press the pedal with his foot to release the steam. When I smiled at him, he would wink at me, but he could scarcely look at me. Every so often he came over, patted me on the back, and then walked away.

I walked over to visit Dot as she finished up a new outfit for my doll. I noticed she had tears in her eyes. "How do you like Kissy's new outfit?" she asked. I touched the frilly dress and stared at the new hat Dot had made for her.

"It's nice," I said, "but Kissy already has a new dress." Dot looked down and kept sewing. She was silent for a while. Then she said, "I know honey, but Dot made her a traveling outfit." I stared as she slipped the dress over my doll's head.

"Okay," I said. I had no clue what a traveling outfit was.

43

When Dot finished, Kissy looked like she was dressed up for Easter. She had on a pretty pink dress with a matching coat and hat. She looked wonderful. I ran over and gave Dot a big hug and kiss and then ran to show Kissy to Dad Hall. He was looking up at the clock on the wall above the front door. He looked sad.

"Look, Daddy," I said. I held the doll up to his face. He stopped the press and smiled at me. The look on his face bothered me; I'd never seen him so down.

"Can I go next door and show the girls?" I asked him. He looked over at Dot; she lowered her head and cleared her work area.

"Not now, baby," he said. "We have to go."

I looked outside. We usually left when the sun went down.

"It's too early to go home," I said, looking over at the pile of clothes. "You're not finished."

Dot got up from her table and put down her glasses. She walked over to me and said, "Come on, honey. You need to get ready."

I watched Dot gather my belongings. When Dad appeared, he had on his gray hat. Dot grabbed me, pulled me close to her, and hugged me real tight. "You be a good girl," she whispered in my ear. Then she walked quickly to the back room.

I looked at Dad Hall. He lowered his eyes toward the ground, took me by the hand, and walked me to the van. As I climbed inside, Mr. Williams, the storeowner next door, stood in the doorway and waved good-bye. He looked sad, and he kept waving as Dad and I drove off.

When we got home, Dad went to his bedroom. They didn't

have a door; there was a plastic partition that slid across on a track. He slid the door shut. Mama Hall was quiet. I could tell she'd been crying. "Baby, I ran you some bathwater," she said. "You need to get ready to go."

I stared at her. "Go where, Mama?" She didn't answer me at first. Instead she went into my bedroom and came back with an outfit.

"Mama, where we going?" I asked.

She started crying. "You're going to see your mother."

Well, that's not bad, I thought. I hadn't seen my mother for a while.

I went into the bathroom and took my bath. It was no big deal to me. The routine was going to be as it always had been. When I finished getting ready, I saw suitcases waiting by the front door. I stared at them.

"Baby, go see your daddy," Mama said.

By now there was a pit in my stomach. I hesitated and then walked into the bedroom. Dad Hall was sitting in his chair, smoking a cigarette and looking out the back window. He called me over and pulled me up on his lap. "You're going to a place called California," he told me. "You and your grandmother are going to take a train so you can see your new home."

I put my head against his chest. "Am I coming right back?" I asked.

Dad was silent for a while. "California is a long way away, but your mother promised that you could come back in the summer," he said.

By then I knew why everyone was sad—I was being taken away. Dad took me by the hand and walked me to Mama. I

45

heard the doorbell ring, and I started to sob. I don't recall who was at the door. It must have been a family member coming to take me to my grandmother's. Mama opened the front door. Screaming, I ran and clung to her waist. Dad Hall began to cry and went back to his bedroom. He couldn't take it.

"Mama, please! Daddy, please!" I begged. "Please don't let them take me, *please*. No! No! No!"

Mama started crying. "Baby, there's nothing we can do. We don't have any say. Your mother wants you to come with her." I felt an excruciating pain inside. I had never seen her cry so hard before. There was agony all over her face. Whoever had come to take me away had to literally drag me. I fell to the floor weeping and screaming, clutching and clawing, trying to grab on to anything sturdy. I got away a couple of times, ran back, and clung to Mama for dear life.

In tears she said, "Baby, please don't cry. You'll see us again. You're coming back to stay for the whole summer. I promise."

Nothing she said made any difference to me. I wanted to die. I had to be picked up and put into the car. I was in the backseat, and as the car drove away, I got on my knees on the seat and looked out the back window. Screaming, I reached my hand toward mama as I watched her get smaller and smaller. I saw her bury her face in her hands and go back in the house. I sobbed uncontrollably.

The next thing I knew, I was on a train with my grandmother. Most of the trip was a blur. The porters were nice to us, but I couldn't smile or enjoy their company. I remember walking to the dining car to eat. The car had large windows everywhere.

In between painful thoughts of the Halls, I looked out the window. The tears continued to flow as I watched the land fly by. I kept picturing Mama and Dad Hall crying; I couldn't get their faces out of my mind. I was more upset about their sadness then my own. Even at that young age, I told myself I could handle it. I didn't want them to suffer because of me.

I had Kissy with me, and I held on to her for dear life. As far as I was concerned, she was all I had. My grandmother was with me, but I felt all alone in the world. I felt no comfort in going to see my mother, either. I wasn't angry with anyone; I didn't know I had the right to be. In order to survive my ordeal, I shut down emotionally, and from then on nothing really mattered.

"You'll like your new home," my grandmother said. "You'll see."

I doubted that very much. I already hated California. I asked my grandmother if Mama Hall was telling the truth about me coming back for the summer. She told me yes. She said my mother had made a solemn promise to the Halls that I would continue to be their daughter.

When we got off the train, my parents drove my grandmother and me around, giving us a tour of San Francisco. My head swiveled from side to side as I drank in the sights. I had never seen anything remotely like the scenery unfolding before my eyes. I braced myself, clutching the seat as we drove up and down steep hills. We drove over a bridge with high triangular shaped cables holding it in place. It was exciting driving over it, yet scary knowing that we were right over the ocean.

It was getting darker, and there were big, looming shadows

47

in the distance. They looked like giants threatening to pounce on the car, but my mother told me they were mountains. Thousands of little white lights seemed to be embedded in them.

"What are those lights inside the mountains?" I asked.

Ari laughed and said, "Those are the houses on the hill. People live there." I couldn't believe it. How had someone climbed way up there and built those houses?

Our new home was an apartment on Wilson Street in a city called Albany, about fifteen miles northeast of San Francisco. Ari was attending Berkeley, and we lived in student housing. There were rows and rows of apartments that looked identical. The area reminded me of maze. I couldn't figure out how people found their way through all those twist and turns.

My losses hit me hard when I saw my new bedroom. I felt sad looking across the hallway at my mother and Ari's room. I was used to sleeping in the same room and bed with my mother, and now I had to sleep by myself. I felt replaced. As I saw it, Ari had come into my life, taken my mother, and turned my entire world upside down. The only comfort I had was that my grandmother didn't go back to Chicago right away. But when she left, the raw wounds reopened, and I went through the trauma of leaving home all over again. My new home was in California, but my heart was not in San Francisco; it was in Chicago.

48

Chapter Four

ON MY OWN

My first day at school demonstrated the pattern of parenting that had been handed down in my mother's family: There was never adequate adult supervision, and older children took up the slack. Back then, of course, I had no way of knowing that the adults I trusted and depended upon for safety and protection were irresponsible. I just thought there was something wrong with me.

My parents had gotten to know one particular couple well, and they asked their daughter Dorothy to walk me to school on my first day. She was supposed to wait for me after school and walk me home. She was in the fourth grade; I was still in second. Dorothy was accommodating but a bit standoffish. I had a gut feeling something was going to go wrong. I didn't want to walk to school with her, but the arrangements were made.

The next day, two girls were standing at my front door. Dorothy introduced my family to her best friend, Lana. They were both going to walk me to school, and unbeknownst to me, Lana wasn't happy about it. She was a territorial little creature. Dorothy was her friend, and Lana had no intentions of sharing her with me. To unsuspecting parents, the girls appeared to be dutiful little angels, but their smiles didn't fool me. I couldn't put my finger on it, but I knew those two were cooking up something and I was going to be the meal. Off I went to a foreign school like a fly between two spiders, alone in the care of two duplicitous fourth-graders. Praise the Lord, my mother slipped a card between the pages of my notebook. It had my name, address, and phone number on it.

We walked to school in silence. My instincts kicked in, and I paid close attention to the route we took. It looked as though we were walking through a park. After we got out of that area, we came to a busy intersection. When we crossed the street, Cornell School was straight ahead. On the way, Lana kept stopping and whispering in Dorothy's ear, and when we got to the front gate of the school, Lana said to me, "Okay, you see those stairs over there?" She pointed straight ahead. I looked in that direction and nodded.

"Good. That's where we'll meet you after school." Lana started walking away. Dorothy said good-bye to her and then helped me find my classroom.

I was afraid to go inside, but I held back the tears and went in. When I walked in, the other children stared at me. My teacher's name was Mrs. Anderson. She was really pretty, but I couldn't believe my eyes. She was pregnant. A teacher having a baby? I didn't even know they went to the bathroom. Mrs. Anderson took me under her wing and introduced me to the class. Eventually they stopped staring and I settled down.

My first day at school went well, but when the bell rang to go home, I got scared. I knew something was up. I walked to the spot where the girls had told me to wait. Mrs. Anderson walked by and asked me if I had a way home. I told her yes. She said, "It's nice having you in our class. I'll see you in the morning." Then she left.

I sat down and waited and waited and waited for the girls. I watched parents pick up their children, and I saw other children walking home in groups or unlocking their bikes to ride home. It wasn't long before everyone was gone, leaving me sitting all alone on the steps. I started to cry. Lana and Dorothy had left me at school. I didn't know what to do. I had paid attention to our route on the way to school, but I didn't know how to find my way all the way back home. It was out of the question to approach a teacher or to go to the office for help. I didn't trust I'd find a nice teacher who would help me. So I sat there for what seemed like an eternity.

My heavenly Father came to my rescue. He sent me an angel in the form of a boy on his bike. He was a white guy about twelve. He saw me crying and walked over to me. "Are you lost?" he asked. I looked up through my tears and nodded.

"Where are you parents?" he asked.

"At home," I said.

We stood there in silence while he looked up and down the street in both directions. I guess he was looking for my family. He asked me more questions. I told him what Dorothy and Lana had done. He asked me if I knew my address or phone number. I handed him the card my mother had given

51

me earlier that day. He looked at it and said, "Come on."

He sat me on the handlebars of his bike and rode me through town. I saw spots I recognized from earlier that day and pointed them out to him. He found my apartment, knocked on the door, and delivered me home safely. My family was elated to see me and thanked the young man profusely.

He walked over to me. "Are you okay?" he asked. Shaken, I told him yes. He left and I never saw him again.

My family took me to Dorothy's house and told her parents what had happened. Dorothy's father called her out of her room, and when she saw us, her eyes widened in horror and she started crying. Her parents made her apologize to me. "I am so sorry. I really am," she sobbed. "It was Lana's idea. I didn't want to do it."

I just looked at her. I was emotionally drained and embarrassed. All I wanted to do was go home and forget everything. Dorothy couldn't play with Lana for a long time. It took a while, but eventually the three of us became friends.

For years I wondered how my family could have entrusted my safety to fourth-graders. It wasn't Dorothy or her family's responsibility to get me to school. I will be forever grateful to the Lord that young man didn't do something awful to me. During that time, a little black girl went missing in the area. They eventually found her body buried beneath a woodpile. I could have been that little girl.

Even though my teachers and classmates were nice to me, I had a hard time adjusting to the schoolwork, which was harder for me in California. I was also hurting all the time and not emotionally present at school. My body sat in my chair, but my mind and spirit drifted aimlessly. To others, I appeared lazy and unmotivated; I just thought I was dumb.

I tried to hide the fact that my schoolwork was suffering. Once I cheated on a test by hiding the answers. Mrs. Anderson caught me, but she gave me a second chance, and I never did it again. Instead, I never took home any papers with bad grades. I brought home only the ones with good grades. I was developing into a little liar.

I never told my family that I was having difficulties, and I acted like everything was fine. So my parents weren't prepared for my report card. When they confronted my teacher, the truth smacked them in the face. She opened her grade book, and there were the bad grades. My parents were humiliated. Ari spanked me only once, and that was the occasion. I wasn't trying to hurt them, but I didn't understand the work, and I didn't want to ask for help. I hid my mistakes out of shame.

53

Education meant everything to Ari; he was truly a genius and got his PhD in his early twenties. All his friends were intellectuals. He loved school and his academic path in life and didn't understand why I had such hard time learning. When my family learned about my failing grades, he tried to help me with my schoolwork, but it didn't go well. The more he tried to help me, the more I shut down.

Ari and I were cut from different cloth. I was a quiet, unassuming child, and people with high IQs and teachers intimidated me. I was only an average student, and I failed miserably in math. Plus, I had way too much on my mind and heart to care anything about school. I never felt a part of my classes. I was imaginative and musically creative, and I found solace in singing and writing stories. I wanted to be a performer, and I wrote movie scripts and plays in class while the teacher taught.

One day a guy in my class named Ken brought his coin collection to school. For no reason at all, I stole his valuable penny and hid it on the floor under a worktable. He was distraught, and the entire class, including me, searched frantically for the coin. I liked Ken a lot, and I planned to return it when the coast was clear. I did, too, but meanwhile I watched him suffer. When no one was looking, I ran and got the penny and told everyone, "Look, I found the penny." I was the hero of the day. Mrs. Anderson was so proud of me, and Ken was so happy that he hugged me.

What an awful thing to do to my classmate! Even at that young age, I asked myself, *What is the matter with me?*

My parents kept their promise and let me go to Chicago for the summers. The time I spent there was wonderful, and when I had to leave, I usually cried the entire four-hour flight home. Then after a few days, I settled back into my routine.

I slowly adjusted to my new life in Albany. As I always had, I sang to keep myself company. My mother had Dinah Washington records, and I performed her entire album *September in the Rain.* My all-time favorite song was "As Long As I'm in Your Arms." I sang Nina Simone songs to my parents and danced to "If I Could Shimmy Like My Sister Kate." I also made friends in our complex, which made life easier. I got along well with the other children. My mother and I were closer, too. I never knew how she felt about all the changes that had taken place in her life, but maybe both of us being away from what was familiar strengthened our bond.

As I faced new people and situations, my mother gave me good advice. She wasn't an intellectual, but she had a lot of common sense and was an excellent judge of character. There weren't too many things she told me that didn't turn out to be right. One of the lessons she constantly instilled in me was to be a leader. She often said, "Lolita, it's easy to follow the crowd; you be a leader." I never forgot her words.

At eight I already exhibited leadership ability, but unfortunately I led a few kids my age in the wrong direction. Some of the ways I interacted with other children were bizarre. I would propose that we find a secret place to play and then suggest that we take off some of our clothing. We didn't touch each other, but we'd look at each other and laugh. It was as if there was a force inside me beckoning to interrupt whatever game we were playing to act out what had happened to me when I played in Chicago. I would come up with these ideas in the middle of playing kickball or jacks. The ideas seemed to pop into my mind out of nowhere. I guess life didn't seem normal to me unless I was involved in some type of seedy, forbidden activity.

Our home was the happening place. My parents entertained a lot, and their guests had great times. It was funny watching the same people who came over to study quietly with Ari dancing to the latest hits, waving towels over their heads, shaking their hips, and laughing and getting down to the

55

beat of the groove. My mother was a lot of fun and quite a hostess. People's roles or titles didn't intimidate her, and she had the ability to make everyone feel welcome. People loved her and felt close to her.

But along with the parties came alcohol, and I noticed that Mom drank quite a bit. When she drank she was fun, but as the night progressed she got stranger and stranger. She became boisterous, danced on tables, and sang loudly. She scared me when she got like that. Those parties were crazy making to me. On the one hand, people were relaxing and having a great time; on the other, some of the married guests ended up in compromising situations. Worse, my mother morphed into a person I didn't know.

The day after a party my mom would sleep in for hours, and when she woke up, she would be quiet and somber. On those mornings I became the little woman of the house. I'd straighten up from the night before and fix my own breakfast, something original like butter and sugar sandwiches, syrup sandwiches, or my own version of French toast—toast burned to a crisp and covered with butter and white sugar.

One day my mother told me something that made me very happy. She said, "You're going to have a little brother or sister soon." I was so happy. I was finally going to have a sibling like my cousins did. The preparations for the baby fascinated me. I watched my parents buy a new white bassinet, little clothes, and all the other things the baby would need. They put everything in my room, as the baby was eventually going to share it. *Oh, how cute,* I thought. *That will be wonderful!* I didn't know what baby brothers or sisters can do to an older sissy. I'd sure find out.

Sam was born in September 1964. My mother said that I was jealous at first. I don't remember that, but I don't doubt it; I was eight and used to being my mother's only child. Deep in my heart, though, after Sam was born I didn't feel alone like before. I truly felt like everyone else—finally. I was also happy when my brother Tufa was born three years later, but I wasn't as naive as I was before Sam was born. *Oh brother, not two of them,* I thought.

Ari never made any distinctions between his sons and me. In fact, he went out of his way to make me a true part of his life. He legally adopted me and gave me his name. Unfortunately, I didn't know how truly loving his actions were. I didn't understand what adoption meant, and it didn't make me feel any closer to him. I stuffed my feelings way down inside and told myself that I didn't care what he thought about me. But I did care.

Each year my parents allowed one of my cousins to come and live with us, and their visits helped me tremendously. On the other hand, I think that having so much company took its toll on my relationship with my mother, as it didn't allow us to spend special time together. We didn't go out to lunch, on shopping sprees, or to the movies together. Our relationship was once again like it had been in Chicago; there was always someone else around.

When I was in third grade, we moved to Madison, Wisconsin, so Ari could attend the university there. I was elated because Madison was closer to Chicago. My parents had never discussed with me the difficulties I experienced moving to

57

California. At the time I didn't think they knew how badly I hurt, but perhaps they did, for they went to great lengths to keep me connected as much as possible with my family. Every weekend we drove home to Chicago.

We stayed in Madison for a year, but I didn't bond with that city at all. The weather was unbearable in the winter, and the curriculum at Spring Harbor School was even harder than at Albany. I felt bad in class because I was the only student the teacher didn't allow to use an ink pen. You had to master cursive and write neatly before you could switch from pencil to pen. I tried really hard, but in the teacher's opinion I never measured up.

She was another teacher who added to my aversion to education, and I emotionally blocked out that school year. I daydreamed all day in class and watched the clock. At eleven-thirty each morning, the milk monitor went to the cafeteria to get the cases of milk for snack time. Waiting for my chocolate milk every day was the highlight of my experience at Spring Harbor. I don't even remember my teacher's name.

What I did learn was that the world doesn't take kindly to people who do sexual stuff with family members. There was a boy in the school name Tim, and the kids whispered that he did nasty things with his little sister. They said that normal people didn't do things like that and called them filthy sickos. I would stare at Tim and his sister when they walked home from school. My stomach churned and I felt sick because I had my own dirty family secrets. If others knew, they would call me a sicko, too. At the age of nine, I felt like a tainted woman. Tim was an older kid, and I stayed clear of him, but

I understood his home life more than I wanted to admit.

Soon it was time to move again. Years later Ari told me that he had had to decide where to go to further his career. He said the choice was between enduring the cold weather or going back to sunny California.

"It wasn't so much an academic choice," Ari said. "I just couldn't stand the cold any longer. I chose California."

He laughed and went on with his conversation, but I thought, *Oh no, you didn't. You did exactly what the Lord wanted you to do. He had a specific plan in mind for our family, and California was part of His plan.*

So it was back to California, this time to beautiful Los Angeles.

59

Chapter Five

RED FLAGS

Ari did very well in his career and was an excellent provider for our family. My parents made sure I attended the best schools wherever we lived. In Los Angeles, I attended Clover Avenue School. I spent more time at Clover, so I was able to develop closer relationships and have a social life. I had neat girlfriends, and we went ice skating, horseback riding, to the movies, and to slumber parties, where we screamed to the music of a new band called The Monkees.

I got so I felt comfortable in Los Angeles, and I graduated from the sixth grade with many fond memories. To my surprise, when I passed my autograph book around, my classmates filled up my book with many endearing sentiments

While I was at Clover Avenue, my music teachers discovered that I could sing, and I started getting solos. My first was the Negro spiritual "Swing Low, Sweet Chariot." I had no idea what that song meant, but people came up to me afterward and told me I did a great job. I was shy and didn't like attention drawn to me, so I didn't like singing solos. I had a pretty voice, but I stood like a statue when I sang and had no show presence at all.

My parents did what they could to help me with my singing and decided to look for a voice teacher. The first one they found gave me a group of songs to learn each week, and the following week I had to pretend I was singing for a live audience. I had to project my voice and use my arms in big, larger-than-life gestures. She wanted me to get ready to audition around town. But I was in no way ready to pursue a musical career. I wasn't competitive or secure enough to even think about going on auditions.

When I was twelve, Ari found me another vocal coach. I began training with Irvin Windward, a prestigious vocal coach who at the time was on the staff of the UCLA music department. I loved him immediately. A wonderfully kind man, he was patient and loving. He saw that I was shy, and he wasn't interested in pushing me into show business. He told my parents that some famous child stars who belted out songs at my age had done major damage to their vocal chords by the time they were adults. He preferred that I work at my own pace and not try to be someone I wasn't. Maybe by the time I was in college, he said, I could pursue a scholarship in opera or musical comedy if I wanted to.

Irvin was more than my voice teacher. He and his wife, Shirley, took me into their hearts and their home. They took me to ballets and other cultural events throughout the city. God used them to meet my need for the extended family I missed terribly, and I studied with Irvin off and on for thirteen years. Today he and Shirley remain a vital part of my life.

At Clover I had another music teacher who took an interest in me. Her name was Geri Haney. With the permission of my family, Ms. Haney took me to her church, and I sang with her choir. She chose songs that fit my voice and taught me the reverence of singing for God. I wore a satin robe and sang traditional inspirational songs. I sang solos for Easter and Christmas services. The church was a big, beautiful Gothic building with stained glass windows, and a lot of celebrities were among the congregation. They introduced themselves to me and cheered me on after I sang.

Irvin Windward gently encouraged me to pursue a singing career, and deep in my heart I had dreams of one day being a famous singer. My goal was to become a professional singer like Diana Ross or Karen Carpenter, but unbeknownst to me, God was using Ms. Haney to get me ready to sing for His kingdom one day.

63

By the time I began middle school, times were good for my family, and we moved into our first house. It was a large, gorgeous colonial, with a terraced yard and lots of land in the back. I had my own bedroom. It was done up in pink and white lace, and I had a white lace canopy bed. I had a doll collection and posters all over my walls, my own record player, and loads of records.

I was a better student in other subjects by then, but I still failed math or got Ds. There was still tension between Ari and me when he tried to tutor me. He couldn't fathom why I had such difficulty, and I clammed up and barely spoke to him. My parents got other people to tutor me in math, but I had a mental block and refused to try.

They tried other ways to reach me. I had guitar, piano, and dance lessons, but none made a lasting impression on me. I was numb and disinterested, and I felt sad all the time. I cried a lot when I was alone. If I was interested in anything, it was in writing songs, children's stories, poetry, and movie scripts. One of my teachers wanted to enter one of my poems in a contest. But I didn't even consider it, for I didn't feel confident enough in myself to compete with others.

Besides, I didn't write stories or sing songs for attention and applause. I did it to escape into the fantasy world I had created. My creativity was my way of purging myself of the pain I felt. One part of me wanted a professional career, but another part wanted seclusion. Songs and stories provided emotional outlets for me, and they were the only area of my life I felt I had control over. I didn't want anyone interfering in my space or putting pressure on me to perform.

I'm sure I appeared unmotivated and ungrateful to my parents and that they felt hurt because I pushed them away. But I wasn't really open to anyone. Not only did I have too much unresolved grief to feel enthusiastic about anything, but I was also entering puberty, which meant I wanted less and less parental involvement anyway. To make matters worse, when I began menstruating, I had cramps so severe that I often ended up in the hospital.

After we'd been in our new home for about a year, my relationship with my mother became war. I was moody and uncommunicative, and she considered my desire for privacy and space disrespectful. I hadn't communicated well as a little girl either, but being a teenager magnified my distance. I didn't want to open up and talk to her.

My parents were still entertaining on a regular basis, and alcohol was a part of it as before, but somehow the partying had taken on an ugly dimension. As the song went, the party was over. I don't remember my mother ever spanking or hitting me when I was little, but from the time I turned twelve she became violent toward me when she drank. She would start out having a good time, but by the end of the party she was a different person.

She would call on me to sing at our functions. I hated performing for guests, and I didn't sing out or do my best. At the end of the night, after everyone had left, my mother would storm into my bedroom, switch on the lights, and accuse me of trying to embarrass her in front of her company. I'd lie in bed feeling terrorized and miserable. As her anger escalated, she'd slap me and say awful things.

Other times, she'd tear into my room, wake me up, and make me clean the kitchen again in the wee hours of the night. The worst part was that I would go downstairs the next morning expecting to get in trouble again, and she'd have no memory of the previous night. She'd call me baby and hug me during the day and tell me how much she loved me. Then after yet another night of drinking, there would be another violent episode.

There was a time when I had enjoyed our parties. Not any longer. I loathed the gatherings and hated to see the preparations begin. I would lie in my bed late at night terrified, waiting for my mother to attack me. I swore to myself that my children would never go through what I endured. I promised myself that they would never see me drunk.

Ari never got involved in our screaming matches. He wasn't violent when he drank, and he didn't bother me personally. He had a temper, but when he got angry, he would get real quiet and throw stuff and slam doors. But now my parents started arguing late at night. I would lie in bed wishing they were downstairs sitting around the dining room table discussing bills. They never argued when they paid bills. I'd pull the covers up over my head and cry. The next morning, no one discussed the previous night's events, and everyone walked around acting like nothing out of the ordinary was going on.

It was crazy making. On the one hand, our family went to Disneyland, parks, and the zoo. We took trips to Las Vegas. The holidays were fun and loaded with toys and goodies. Then there were those horrible parties and fights. Our home was becoming unhappy and unstable, and I never knew when the other shoe was going to drop.

It didn't help matters at all that when my grandmother came to visit, she introduced us to the occult. Her fascination with other cultures had stimulated her interest in metaphysical phenomena, and she was reading books about fortune-telling, tea reading, ESP, meditation, and astral traveling. Her obsession with mysticism eventually led us to an ESP lab and its leader. I don't know how it started, but every week we attended meetings.

My cousins Moe and Chief were living with us at the time. Moe was sixteen, Chief was fifteen, and I was fourteen. I didn't consider myself part of the leader's following, and I never practiced any of the rituals. I was there because my family took me there. At first, Moe, Chief, and I thought it was all a bunch of hogwash, and we laughed about it all the time. But it didn't seem so funny when I saw the effect it had on our family.

The leader and his wife taught us how to meditate on different colors of light to attract the energy they generated. Blue was for creativity, green was for money, and orange was for wisdom. We all wanted to see each other's auras, the glowing lights of energy that supposedly surrounded us all. They indoctrinated us into white witchcraft and taught us how to leave our bodies and allow good spirits to enter them. When the lights went down and the leader took our group through the strange exercises, I prayed under my breath for God's protection. I didn't know God personally then, but I knew something wasn't right about what we were doing.

After a while, my family started visiting mediums and psychics. I went on occasion. Every one of them told me things about my life that no one knew. I thought it was neat that those people had such gifts. I saw that there was power in the invisible realm and thought we were entertaining loving, good spirits. I didn't know then about familiar spirits and how they seduce and deceive people.

What I did know was that our home was getting darker and darker, and the more we attended those meetings, the scarier they became. Some of the followers allowed themselves to be spirit guides for unknown forces. Their voices changed as spirits entered their bodies and they gave the group messages. Then one night I had a horrible dream that our house was engulfed in flames. It crumbled and burned to the ground. I woke up terrified. I didn't know what it meant. My family was ignorant and blind; we had no idea we had opened the door to hell in our lives.

After elementary school, I lost contact with the friends I had made and had to start all over. The little bit of security my school had provided disappeared. When I was in middle school, or junior high, as it was called in those days, I was bused to two different communities. The first school was by the Los Angeles International Airport. They eventually closed the school because of the noise, and I began attending Palms Junior High.

In seventh grade, I had my first boyfriend. His name was Duane, and he was one year ahead of me. He was a handsome black guy with green eyes, and he was the perfect gentleman. My relationship with him was pure and innocent. I was shy and never would have dreamed of approaching any guy. Duane knew I was frightened, so he took his time and walked me to class every day until I warmed up to him. He was kind and loving and never suggested anything inappropriate or disrespectful. I liked him a lot, but I felt panicky and unsure of myself whenever he was around. I didn't know how to relate to him. I had an awful time being at ease and acting natural.

I watched the other young couples on the campus. The girls would sit at the cafeteria tables laughing and talking with their boyfriends while they ate lunch, but I felt ashamed and embarrassed every time Duane sat next to me. I could never eat my lunch in front of him. One afternoon I got to the cafeteria first. I was famished, and I tried to get my food and hurry up and eat it before Duane got there. My cousin Moe was eating lunch with me. When I saw Duane approaching, I jumped up. I was about to rush to the trash can to throw my food away when Moe stopped me.

"Girl, you crazy?" he said. "Give me that food!" He grabbed my sandwich, stuffed it in his mouth, and cleared the other items off my tray in nothing flat. I just looked at the bread crumbs on his mouth.

"I'll meet you here tomorrow if you don't want your food," he said, and off he went to fraternize with his buddies.

I was relieved the food was gone, even though I went through the entire day starving. *Why can't you just relax and talk to the boy?* I often asked myself.

The problem was that I didn't want Duane to know I was human. If we were walking together, I wouldn't even let him know when I needed to use the restroom. I hid all of my needs, just like I hid all of my mistakes. I didn't want him to get too close to me because I was sure he'd see my flaws. If he thought I was strange, he never treated me differently. He remained loving and supportive. Duane attended a different high school than I did, so we eventually went our separate ways.

I met other guys on my summer visits to Chicago. I had two other boyfriends over a span of two years. Both were friends of Moe.

One was named Eddie. He was worldlier than Duane. He drank beer and told me he smoked weed, but for some reason I didn't have the same problem relating to him as I had with

Duane. Eddie felt familiar to me. He had problems at home. He was nice to me, but not as gentle and protective as Duane had been. He hung out with biker friends and was into martial arts. Eddie taught me how to really kiss, and he wanted to take our relationship to another level, but I wasn't willing. I had to fight him off on many dates. He stopped when I said no, but he wasn't pleased about it.

I knew what my role was in Eddie's life: I was there to watch over him and make sure he didn't go off the deep end. I was always counseling him not to drink, or to go home and tell his mother where he was going. I was his little mother, his rescuer. Duane, on the other hand, didn't need rescuing. He came from a good family, didn't drink or do drugs, and did well in school. He was a healthy young man. I was used to troubled individuals. Unfortunately, I wasn't able to rescue Eddie soon enough. A few years later, he was found shot to death on the streets. No one ever discovered who killed him.

My second boyfriend was named Dee. He, too, was kind and loving to me. He treated me wonderfully. I liked him a lot, but again, I didn't know how to relate to him. I was quiet a lot of the time. Dee was a mature sixteen; he worked and went to school. He didn't need emotional repairing. I felt out of my league with him.

A year later, I met a third young man back home in Los Angeles. His name was Michael. He was in trouble with the law for doing drugs. I loved him deeply and felt a kindred spirit to him. By then there was a clear and ominous pattern in how I related to the opposite sex: I didn't feel deep, burning passion for guys who were kind and decent and peaceful. Instead, I felt detached, sad, and even bored.

Chapter Six

BEVERLY HILLS HIGH

When I graduated from Palms Junior High, my parents sold our house and moved so I could attend Beverly Hills High, a prestigious, highly acclaimed high school. You had to live in the area or have a permit to go there. There was a long list of outsiders waiting to get permits, so my parents found an apartment in the neighborhood right across the street from the campus. However, a lot of repairs and painting needed to be done, and we couldn't move in right away. So for one semester of my sophomore year I attended the famous Los Angeles High, where they used to film the television show *Room 222*.

I wasn't at Los Angeles High long enough to make friends, and the new school I was getting ready to attend included the ninth grade. This meant that the majority of kids at Beverly Hills High had a year's head start to get settled in. In addition, most of the students lived in the area and had gone through elementary and junior high together.

By that time, I had already attended eight different schools. I wasn't happy about the move and had a bad attitude. My parents put a lot of effort into getting me into that elite school, and they thought I was ungrateful. However, my mood didn't come from lack of gratitude. It came from insecurity and my fear of once again having to face the unknown. It was hard starting all over and making new friends. I was always coming into the middle of situations that already existed. It was painfully lonely always being an outsider, the new girl on the block.

I don't think Ari realized how hard all the moves and adjustments were on me. He had left his family when he was very young to get his education in a foreign country. He had goals, and taking full advantage of the opportunities afforded him, he put his hand to the plow and kept going until he reached every single one of them. I guess he figured that I would do the same, but the truth was that I just didn't have the emotional fortitude he did.

Just looking across the street at that beautiful school intimidated me. My attitude came across as nonchalant, but I was terrified. My challenges in the past had been to fit in emotionally and sometimes racially. At this school, it was a whole new game, and this time the rules involved prominence, privilege, and prestige. My schoolmates included the children of Dean Martin, Don Knotts, Don Adams, Stanley Kramer, Tony Curtis and Janet Leigh, Rosemary Clooney, Diana Ross, Greg Morris, Barry Gordy, Dino De Laurentiis, Debbie Reynolds, and Florence Henderson. There were the children of politicians, producers, songwriters, doctors, and lawyers. And those were just the ones I knew about. Believe me, there were more.

Not every student who attended the school was rich or had famous parents, but the atmosphere was definitely elitist. To say the least, it was an adjustment to watch some of my fellow students driving to school in Jaguars, Porsches, and Mercedes. Ari was a prominent professor by that time, so I didn't exactly come from the salt mines, but emotionally I didn't feel part of the elite. Ari was the one with the awesome credentials and a bright future, not me.

Fortunately, race was not an issue with the students and the majority of the staff. I had had some problems involving race in the past, and it had been hard to move from a black neighborhood in Chicago to a predominatcly white environment in California. But it was, after all, the seventies. Many black kids attended the high school, and interracial couples strolled the campus. When I arrived, no one either welcomed me or mistreated me. I was just another student, which was a relief. The only problem I had was in the music department.

In the past, music had always been a way for me to fit in and eventually make new friends. That wouldn't be the case in this school. I always joined the school choir or the girl's glee, so I wanted to audition for the Madrigals. I approached Mr. Harper, but he told me in a not-so-kind tone, "We don't need any more voices." Then he walked away.

By that time I had met a few students at the school, and Fran, one of my new white friends, told me, "That's not so. I auditioned at the beginning of the week."

Some of the other white students said that Mr. Harper was prejudiced. This was new experience for me. Even though I had been uprooted from an all-black environment and thrust into a white one when we moved to California, I had never before had a teacher reject me because of my color. I went home and told my parents. They contacted the school and found out that Mr. Harper had indeed been auditioning for the Madrigal Singers. He was forced to give me an audition with my parents present.

At first he told my family that he didn't want me to feel bad, but that his singers were more traditional. Ari informed him that I had been trained to sing opera and musical comedy. When I finished my audition, Mr. Harper was speechless. He looked embarrassed and didn't know what to say. His male assistant was present when I sang. He winked at me and gave me the thumbs-up behind Mr. Harper's back. Mr. Harper said, "You're a very good singer."

I was proud of the fact that I had done so well under pressure, and I was looking forward to singing with the group. Mr. Harper had been with the school for years, and the Madrigals had won many competitions. I don't know what happened, but he still didn't allow me to sing with the group. I can only imagine that he put his foot down and absolutely refused to have me in his class. I guess if the choice was between keeping Mr. Harper happy or me happy, the school went with him. They did nothing to press the issue further.

I made my peace with the situation. I didn't like Mr. Harper, and I reached the point that I didn't want to go back. I knew it and so did Mr. Harper, and I didn't try out for any

74

other music groups. I took an acting class, but the theater department was also a tight-knit group, and I was competing with famous names. I gave up on the hope of finding my niche in the performing arts department.

God once again sent a woman to hear me sing. Her name was Sandy. I don't remember what job she had at the school, but she wanted me to be in a talent show for a benefit. I went to her house every week and practiced. She was very support-ive and proud of me. I did that benefit for her and was grateful for her kindness and acceptance. I met other interest-ing people through her, but that was the extent of my singing at Beverly Hills High.

While I was practicing for the talent show, my grandmother came to visit us. She was in bad health due to poor circula-tion. She'd had a tracheotomy some months earlier, and it was very taxing on her whenever someone had to suction the mucous from her throat with a tube. The night before my per-formance, she said, "I won't be dealing with this trach much longer." Looking back, I think my grandmother was saying good-bye to us.

When I got home from the talent show, everything was solemn. My mother was distraught. Earlier my grandmother had had difficulty breathing, and they had tried to suction her and put the trach back in, but they couldn't. They summoned the paramedics, but to no avail. My grandmother died that evening while I was singing.

I was sixteen at the time, and never in my life had I known such agony. My grandmother had always been very loving toward me, and I'd never before lost anyone so close to me. Every time I saw her glasses in their case, I would picture her relaxing in her favorite chair and writing in her journal, and I would fall apart. I cried for two weeks straight. I didn't go back to Chicago for the funeral, but my parents did. When my mother returned home, she had to be escorted off the airplane in a wheelchair. She could hardly function and was despondent for months.

Life at home continued to be unbearable. After Grandmother's death, my mother became even more combative. I walked on eggshells trying not to make waves, but somehow the waves kept crashing in anyway. Her drinking was escalating, as were her verbal and physical assaults. When she drank, she accused me of doing things I wasn't doing. She told me that "everything" was my fault, and I believed her. I started fighting back and saying awful things to hurt her. Ugly changes were taking place in my soul.

After our arguments, I felt ashamed and guilty and responsible for her. I felt I was the cause of the chaos and tension in our home. I thought maybe if I were a better daughter, a better student, or a better person, she wouldn't be treating me as she was. I truly believed that I was the source of all my mother's pain and frustration.

I wasn't numb as I had once been. I felt emotional pain and distress every single day. The only way I can describe the agony I lived in is to say that my heart throbbed all the time. I tried to muster up the courage to take my own life. I got a bottle of over-the-counter sleeping tablets, and twice after a heated argument with my mother, I tried to swallow them to end it all. But I was terrified of where my soul would go if I succeeded. We weren't attending church and were still seeking the advice of mediums and psychics, but I knew that God forbade suicide. I cried in despair because I didn't have the courage to take the pills.

At school I pretended that I was happy and never discussed my home life. I didn't think I had the right to tell anyone what I was feeling, and I worked hard not to show how angry I was or make anyone else angry. As I saw it, my job was to listen and take instruction. I even started trying to understand my mother and other angry souls by counseling them and becoming their confidante.

I had discovered that the only way I found acceptance and a little bit of peace was to placate stronger personalities and to be needed by them. I began to take responsibility for people emotionally. My job was to fix the broken and advise, comfort, and rescue the lost. I got acceptance from others when they depended on me for comfort, but then I became resentful and felt used. My role was martyr and savior. Unfortunately, there was no one in my life to save and rescue me.

Neat things began to happen in my junior year. William, one of the most popular football players, started liking me. We talked on the telephone for hours at night, and he gave me his letter jacket to wear at school. I couldn't believe it—I was in! I was the girlfriend of a football player, and a lot of girls liked him.

A few girls in my English class wanted to nominate me for homecoming princess. I pleaded with them not to submit my name. I was certain that I didn't know enough people to be voted in. They didn't do it, but I was so grateful to them for thinking that I had what it took to be a princess. William had enough clout to place as a prince, but he wasn't interested in being in the homecoming court.

When I started hanging around with homecoming princesses and cheerleaders, I finally found my role at school—acting like a mother to some of my troubled friends. I didn't see myself as pretty and charismatic, so I hid behind those who were. My new friends were doing things I never had the nerve to do, like attending parties and sneaking out of the house to visit college boys. So I lived my life vicariously through them. I sat back and watched them enjoy themselves. Sometimes they got themselves in trouble, and when they did, I rescued them. I stood by and comforted friends who had abortions, nursed back to health those recovering from hangovers, and kept the secrets of the drug takers.

My parents and William's parents were close friends. They visited on the weekends, so William and I spent a lot of time together. I took his little sister around with my brothers and me all the time. It was a great time. His parents really liked me and were glad their son was dating me. Being accepted and a part of the general scene was a welcome change.

Then one night I found out that William had gone out with another girl at school. It was a known fact that she had loose morals. I wasn't sexually active in high school and couldn't understand. My mother tried to help me, but she couldn't do anything except be there. William was my first broken heart. We had been going together for more than a year, and I really cared for him. I laid my head in my mother's lap and sobbed.

Ari hugged me, and we had a long father-daughter talk. He told me that if a man truly wanted to control himself sexually, he could. "Never settle for someone cheating on you," he said. "There is no excuse for that type of disrespect." That helped me tremendously. I still cherish that special moment with him. My parents lovingly helped me through that ordeal. William and I went our separate ways, but we remained friends.

When I was a senior, another double-faced molester crossed my path. Fortunately, I knew the ropes by then. He didn't get to me, but he hurt a close friend of mine. This man was a charming, charismatic forty-five-year-old actor who was married to a dear friend of my parents. He went to the high school sports events and hung out with my friends and me. I didn't know he was trying to get close to me by meeting my friends.

One evening after a basketball game, he tried to get me to go to his apartment, but I wasn't interested in going. I didn't think it was a big deal then because I was seventeen and thought I was grown and could handle his attention. I introduced him to my girlfriend Fran at a game. Unbeknownst to me, he wooed her to his apartment and began sleeping with her. It became an awful mess. I blew the whistle on them, and when his wife found out, she divorced him. I felt guilty for the affair because I had introduced him to Fran, and I lost a very dear girlfriend in the process. Fran didn't speak to me for years.

I thought only little girls could be molested. I had no idea my friend was being abused. I wasn't going to be molested anymore. No man was ever going to touch me unless I wanted him to. What I didn't know was that sexual molestation has a life all its own. I labored under the assumption that as a woman, I would be in control of all my relationships. How wrong I was.

Most of the friends I made at Beverly Hills High were either a year behind me or a year ahead of me. I had only three fairly close associates in my class. After I graduated in 1973, I never attended any of my high school reunions because I figured no one would know who I was. Out of a graduating class of three hundred, I would have been shocked if I had recognized four people.

Nevertheless, by the time I graduated I liked my school. The curriculum was one of the most challenging in the state, and except for math, I got good grades and wasn't struggling like before. Apparently Beverly Hills High prepared me more than I realized. I probably could have gone to college. My SAT scores weren't high, but they weren't terribly low either. I just didn't feel competent enough to contact colleges. The only educated people around me attended major universities. It was all or nothing in my thinking. It didn't even dawn on me to try a smaller campus or a musical academy.

High school was over and my future awaited. The only problem was that I had no idea what I wanted to do with my life. At eighteen, I was like a defective piece of pottery that had been shaped in a flawed family mold. Now the focus of my story was about to change from the glaring flaws of my family to my own conspicuous failings. My life was now in my own hands. Unfortunately, they were the hands of a neglected, abused little girl, and they would shatter an already marred vessel.

PART II

Child in Control

POSSIBILITIES

Fanny Levin

With haze there is clarity,
with darkness there is light,
with sadness there is laughter,
with day there is night.

With ego there's humility,
with control there's letting go,
with upset there is peace,
with resistance there is flow.

With bondage there is freedom,
with isolation—unity,
with void there is completeness,
with confusion—certainty.

With denial there's acceptance,
with pretension there is truth,
with confinement there's release,
with adulthood there is youth.

God is our possibilities,
believe…dreams do come true!
broaden your horizons,
His potential lives
within me—and you.

Chapter Seven

A NEW FAMILY

During my senior year, I had babysat to make money and used my earnings to take acting lessons. I found an agent and went on auditions, and I almost got hired for a television situation comedy. I got three callbacks, but in the end the director chose a girl with more experience. I went on more auditions, but I was afraid to hustle for another part, and I let the acting go. I didn't have enough confidence to step out in another direction, and by the time I graduated, I felt beaten down and lost.

My magic solution was to get married. I bought into the lie that having a family of my own would save me from myself. Stability and security were major issues for me, and I thought that having a husband and children would provide the structure my life was missing. So I floundered around trying to keep myself busy until I met my "soul mate." I truly thought that my desire for marriage was healthy—no different than what every other young woman yearned for.

Because my life had been so unstable while I was growing up, I lacked internal structure, and I had a very hard time knowing what do to with my spare time after I graduated from high school. School had provided routine, structure, and order for me. Now I didn't know what to do with myself. I didn't have the inner resources I needed to be able to take care of myself emotionally, and I felt anxious, like a little girl lost in a big city without her parents. To make matters worse, my parents weren't getting along at all. It seemed there was no security anywhere.

My back was up against a wall. I had to decide what to do soon because Ari was going on a sabbatical for year, and my parents and brothers were supposed to leave for Europe in a few months. They invited me to go, but I couldn't handle being uprooted again. Moving from one state to another had been bad enough; I wasn't about to go to another country.

I finally decided to go to Los Angeles City College—for what reason, God only knew. My mother helped me get settled in a studio apartment, and Ari was going to pay the rent while they were gone. I had no idea what major or minor to pursue. Music was the love of my life, but it never dawned on me to make music or theater my major. I took one music class to learn how to read music, but I eventually dropped it.

A friend of mine from high school also ended up at City College, and she decided to major in sociology. Since I had no direction, I declared a major in sociology as well. For a few months, I felt a little better. I had an apartment and I was in school. Soon, however, I was walking around the campus depressed and unfocused. I didn't belong in sociology. I was wasting precious time and money.

Then a bomb hit our family. Ari told my mother that he no longer wanted to be in the marriage and went to Europe alone, leaving my mother and two younger brothers behind. My mother was shattered to the core. I was at a point in my life when I was struggling to find my own way and identity, but I had to put my life on hold and help my mother and little brothers adjust to the painful changes they were facing.

I put a further wedge between Ari and me by taking it upon myself to confront him about the situation, though it wasn't my place to get involved in their affairs. I found myself in a difficult position. I knew how hard it was to live with my mother, but Ari wasn't always easy to live with either. I took my mother's side as I always had and said very hurtful things to Ari. I considered my relationship with him basically over.

All my plans now changed. My parents had moved into another house after I graduated, but they had sold it when they were getting ready to leave for Europe. Ari put my mom and two brothers in a one-bedroom apartment not far from mine. Since he wasn't going to pay my rent any longer, I moved in with them. My mother had had a few part-time jobs over the years, but she had no career and no way to support herself. Ari did make some provisions for her and my brothers, but it wasn't enough to live on, and I had to work to help.

I went to a temporary agency looking for work, but since I wasn't trained in any profession, I ended up in boring, dead-end jobs. I eventually landed a full-time position as a stock girl in a trendy boutique. I was bored to tears and cried every day in the fitting rooms. The boutique manager was a doll.

85

She knew that being a stock girl was a drag and gave me a shot at being a salesgirl, but I didn't have enough confidence to approach people to sell them anything, so I remained a stock girl.

The future looked dark and gloomy. I felt I would never have the opportunity to live my own life. At home all was sadness and despair. I felt terrible for my mother. Emotionally, I became the head of the family, and my little brothers clung to me for dear life. To escape the pain, I began to drink wine at night. At least there was finally peace between my mother and me. We were both too depressed to fight about anything.

Then one day the phone rang. Some time before my parents split up, I had gone on an audition for a job singing in an all-girl group. Months had passed, and I hadn't heard a word. Now someone was calling to tell me I had been chosen as the fourth singer in the group. We had a record deal with Warner Brothers and were going to record a country song. The manager wanted to call us Four Broad Nights, a spoof of the band Three Dog Night. I felt uncomfortable with the name because it sounded disrespectful, but I had almost no sense of personal worth, so I was elated to be in their band. I signed a contract for seven years.

As it turned out, the entire thing suddenly came to an abrupt halt. I have no idea what eventually happened to the band. Unbeknownst to me, God was orchestrating my path, and it was never His will for me to be in that group. He just wanted me to meet Tara, who would introduce me to her boyfriend Rick, a musician who performed with the New Christy Minstrels. Rick suggested that I audition for Sid

Garrison, the owner. I did and Sid liked me, but he still had to audition other young artists throughout the country. I really wanted to go on tour with that group, so I anxiously waited to hear from him.

When I didn't hear anything, I became depressed. To get through the rest of the day after work, I would sit on the bathroom floor with my back up against the tub, drink, and cry. Meanwhile, God had sent an angel to help my mother. Gloria had successfully weathered her own crises and understood what my mother was going through. She took my mother under her wing and started taking her to Bible studies. I had no idea where my mother was going on certain evenings, but I definitely saw a transformation taking place in her life.

One afternoon after one of my bathroom episodes, I crawled into bed and took a nap. Not long afterward, my mother woke me up. She had a peaceful smile on her face.

"I have something wonderful to share with you," she said.

I looked at her as if she'd lost her mind. I was used to her crying or moping around the house looking disoriented. I had never seen her so peaceful. I sat up, frightened. I didn't trust her new behavior yet. She started telling me where she'd been going evenings.

"I asked Jesus into my heart last night," she said. "I want you to have Him in your heart, too." I just looked at her in confusion. I knew who Jesus was, but I had no idea what it meant to have Him in my heart.

"Doesn't everyone already have Him?" I asked her.

She explained that you had to invite Jesus into your life, and then she gave me a pamphlet to read. It was about the four spiritual laws. I looked it over, but it made no sense to me. She got her Bible and read Revelation 3:20: "I stand at the door and knock. If anyone hears my voice and opens the door, I will come in and eat with him, and he with me." She said that in her Bible study she'd been learning that Jesus is a gentleman. He never forces His will on anyone. We have to give Him permission to work in our lives.

Then she asked me the strangest question. "Do you want to be born again and enter the kingdom of God?" She showed me John 3:3, where Jesus told Nicodemus that he had to be born again to see the kingdom of God. "Do you want to say the sinner's prayer and ask Jesus into your heart and be born again?" she asked.

My mother told me how much joy and peace she felt inside since she had given her heart and life to the Lord. The burden of the past months had been lifted. I saw the change in her countenance, and I wanted the same peace and assurance. "Yes," I said, "I want to say the prayer."

Before I began, she showed me more Scriptures to let me know what God's Word had to say. She didn't want me to take her word alone. I read John 3:16: "God so loved the world that he gave his one and only Son, that whoever believes in him shall not perish but have eternal life." Then I read Romans 10:9–10: "If you confess with your mouth, 'Jesus is Lord,' and believe in your heart that God raised him from the dead, you will be saved. For it is with your heart that you believe and are justified, and it is with your mouth that you confess and are saved."

Then my mother read the prayer on the back of the pamphlet, and I repeated the lines after her. I confessed that I was a sinner and needed to be cleansed from my unrighteousness. I wanted to be released from the hold that Satan had on my life. I believed that Jesus was the Savior and that He died on the cross for my sins. I prayed the prayer and asked Jesus to be Lord of my life. At the age of nineteen, I told Jesus how much I loved Him and that I wanted to be born again.

My mother and I talked about our involvement in occult practices. She turned to the book of Isaiah and read:

> All the counsel you have received has only worn you out! Let your astrologers come forward, those stargazers who make predictions month by month, let them save you from what is coming upon you. Surely they are like stubble; the fire will burn them up. They cannot even save themselves from the power of the flame. Here are no coals to warm anyone; here is no fire to sit by. (47:13–14)

In this passage, Isaiah says that the end of people who put their trust in magic spells and sorceries will be calamity and catastrophe. When I saw those verses, I remembered the dream I'd had years earlier about our house burning to the ground. I lowered my head in repentance before the Lord for dabbling in the occult and asked His forgiveness for my ignorance.

Bells and whistles didn't go off, and I didn't have a visit from angels or anything like that, but I felt a heavenly presence in the room. I started crying. I felt peaceful and warm inside. I had been distraught when I went to sleep earlier, but after I received the Lord, my mind became clear, and I felt clean and refreshed. I couldn't believe that the God of the universe loved me.

We are all, to one extent or another, broken people. That's why God sent His Son to earth—to mend us—and the very first way He does that is to save us through His Son. Until that happens, nothing else can. Once you put your trust in Him, He places you in His family—gives you brothers and sisters in Christ to support you—and then the Holy Spirit begins to teach you about Him through His Word so that you can learn to trust Him.

When I received Jesus as my Savior, I meant every word of it. I loved Jesus as much as I was capable of loving Him. However, I didn't really know Him, and it's impossible to truly love and trust someone you don't know well. So although I was saved, it would be a very long time before I began to allow the Lord to rule in my life.

I started attending the Bible studies while I waited to hear from the Christy Minstrels. I didn't know what to expect when I went for the first time, but I was overwhelmed with the joy and love I felt there. There were about twenty people present that evening, and I was surprised to see so many young people there on a Friday night.

They were from all different walks of life. Some had come out of the hippie movement; some were former drug users; and others had extensive backgrounds in the occult, satanism, Transcendental Meditation, astrology, and witchcraft. They were old and young, rich and poor, black and white, Native American, Hispanic, messianic Jew, Catholic, Baptist, Buddhist, and Methodist. A lot of them were in some form of show business.

Those were the days of a revival known as the "Jesus Movement," and some mainline churches were doing an about-face. Many of God's people were no longer accepting dead religious traditions; they were hungering and thirsting for more of Him. My new brothers and sisters in Christ were peaceful, loving, accepting individuals. No one cared if you worshiped in blue jeans, shorts, muumuus, or evening gowns. The emphasis was on the heart, and our common dominator was Jesus Christ. We wanted to be like our heavenly Father, and we didn't judge others by their appearance or fail to respect those who continued to worship Him in a more traditional manner.

God met His broken people right where they were, opened His arms, and loved them. Our assistant pastor, Brent Rue, once said, "God catches His fish before He cleans them." Eventually, in His time and His way, God would make the necessary changes in each of us. As my own journey began, I saw that God was not concerned that we were marred vessels; He just wanted willing vessels. He would manage the tedious process of mending and shaping each life. I was discovering daily that God was real and not a cold, disinterested tyrant who rejected you if you lost your way. As I stumbled, tumbled, and fumbled to grow in my faith, I would find out just how patient and long-suffering He truly is.

I was used to attending services where preachers either screamed and pounded on the podium or were so deadly dull that I thought I was in a mausoleum. Our pastor, Kenn Gulicksen, wasn't that way. His approach to teaching Scripture was gentle and loving. We didn't have to take everything he said at face value. He was always open to questions and a peaceful debate. God had also blessed him with a beautiful singing voice, and it was truly heavenly to sing along with him and our praise and worship leader, Keith Green. They played their guitars and taught us sacred songs, and with lifted hands we sang and gave praises to our Lord.

At one of these Bible studies, Gloria introduced me to Jill Miller, coauthor of the song "Let There Be Peace on Earth." Because the song was known the world over, Jill met many different people from all faiths and walks of life. She was loved on a grand basis, but also judged and criticized. I don't think people understood her at times. Jill wasn't your conventional senior citizen or believer. She marched to the beat of her own drum. She was a free spirit, not affected by others' preconceived notions of who she was or should be.

Jill was also an intensely private woman. She wasn't fond of company and rarely let anyone besides family members spend the night with her. However, she felt safe and comfortable with me, and I spent many nights fellowshipping with her. We understood each other's need for privacy. Even when I stayed at her place, I kept to myself. We visited and talked and ate dinner, but otherwise I preferred reading or taking naps in my room while she took care of her personal affairs. On more than one occasion she told me that she didn't feel she had to entertain me, and it pleased her that her notoriety wasn't the reason I was her friend. I knew that Jill, too, was battling deep hurts, and we found comfort in each other's company and prayers.

Jill never gave pat answers for the suffering in life. Her heart was sensitive to the deep needs of others, but she had insights that many people weren't privy to. I think she was way ahead of the game. She saw where the church was lacking in terms of reaching the lost, but when she tried to explain the vision she had from the Lord, no one understood what she was saying.

She often said to me, "We need to have people centers on every corner." She envisioned these centers as coffee shops where the lonely could go and talk about mutual subjects of interest or share their pain. Volunteers would lend listening ears to those who came. "I would love to have a place to go and rest and visit, without someone immediately shoving Scriptures down my throat at the front door," she said. "There would be time for sharing Scriptures later."

Jill knew that many people who desperately needed healing would never set foot in a church or a therapist's office. The people centers would be places where they could reach out for help and support. Jill was convinced that that's the way our Savior ministered to people. He walked and ate and fellowshipped with the broken before He recruited disciples. Jesus wasn't interested in passing out clichéd, generic answers to those who followed Him. He saw individuals, not masses.

Jill never pried into my affairs, though she knew I was struggling emotionally, trying not to go over the edge. I believe having the Lord in my life saved me from a nervous breakdown. I was battling debilitating depression. There were days when I could scarcely eat or concentrate. I felt sad and hopeless, and not hearing from the Christies intensified my anxiety. I felt that if that door didn't open, I had no hope of ever escaping the rut I was in.

One evening, despondent over the lack of direction in my life, I was wrapped in one of Jill's warm afghan blankets, sipping a cup of hot cocoa and lamenting my fate. "God brought you too far to drop the ball now," Jill said. "When it's time for an answer, you'll have one, and it will be the right one."

I felt better. We had dinner and were watching a movie when the phone rang. Jill answered it and handed me the receiver.

"You're in the Christies!" my mother screamed from the other end of the line.

I jumped up and down and shouted, "Jill, I made it! I made it!"

"I knew it all the time," she said with a smile.

Chapter Eight

ON THE ROAD

I was elated that I had been chosen out of so many hopefuls. An impressive list of stars had once traveled with the Christies, including Barry McGuire, Kenny Rogers, Karen Black, and John Denver. I couldn't believe this was happening to me.

During the ensuing months, there were serious rehearsals at Sid's studio on Beverly Boulevard. Two other new girls, Wendy and Karen, and I were replacing three girls who had been on tour for a long time and wanted to go home. I was nervous because we were joining four guys who had done the tour for quite a while. This meant that we new girls had to get our routines down pat.

I rehearsed during the day and continued attending Bible studies in the evening. Our group was growing fast and beginning to take shape as a church. Pastor Kenn sought the Lord diligently for direction, and he felt that it was time for us to name our church. We all wrote down our suggestions, and about a month later we voted on the strongest names submitted. We unanimously decided on "the Vineyard."

The Vineyard became my spiritual home and family, and I am proud of the fact that my mother and I were among the original members of such a beautiful, strong church. For the first time in my life, I was right in the heart of a new beginning. I wasn't the new kid on the block or an outcast, and I didn't have to struggle to fit into an already established situation.

Soon it came time for me to join the other Christies on the road. The night before I left, one of my dear brothers from the Vineyard took me out for pizza. His name was John Smalley. John told me about the challenges he was facing in his personal life, including some important decisions he had to make soon. He sent me off with hugs, support, and prayers that I would have a wonderful time away. John was a dear friend, and I was glad he prayed for me because I had a hard time leaving to go on tour.

I was to fly out and meet the band the next day in Bloomington, Indiana. When it came time to leave for the airport, my eleven-year-old brother Sam, upset about my leaving, turned his head away and walked quietly into the bedroom. I had a flashback to the expression on Mama Hall's face when I was taken away from her home, and a deep pain stabbed me in the heart. Knowing Sam was sad, I started to cry. Suddenly I was once again the little seven-year-old girl who had been torn away from Chicago years earlier.

Our tour manager was on the same plane, and he must have thought something was seriously wrong with me because I cried the entire trip with the same intense pain I had felt as a child. The trouble was that I wasn't seven. I was nineteen, but I couldn't stop crying. I wanted to go back home to the Vineyard. A little girl, not a grown woman, was traveling to join the New Christy Minstrels.

I arrived in Indiana and met the other members of the group. They greeted the new grunts graciously, and we all got along well. The guys were professionals and excellent performers. They were nice to us, but we were replacing very talented ladies, and they expected us to do our jobs. Karen was a former beauty queen from upstate New York, with a beautiful smile and a tender heart. Wendy was a sweet, redheaded fireball. She could belt out a song like Winona Judd, and she loved Elvis Presley and sang like him. I sang light jazz and rhythm and blues.

97

The only person I had any problems with was the banjo player. I was taken back by his hostility toward me. He attacked Christianity and teased me by saying awful things about the Bible. He constantly cracked jokes about Jesus and mocked me for being weak and needing religion. I didn't know what to do. I was a new believer, and I wasn't aware that everybody didn't love Jesus.

I kept my distance from the banjo player, but I was hurt. I couldn't figure out why anyone would make fun of God, especially since He humbled himself by taking the form of man and then hung on a cross for our sins. *What a beautiful display of love God showed mankind,* I thought. I was relieved when the banjo player decided to leave the tour. God sent another very talented banjo player, and he became my closest buddy. I trusted and respected Scott, and he treated me like a sister.

The Christies toured fifty weeks out of the year. We put on shows in school auditoriums in small towns and in civic auditoriums in larger cities. We performed at state fairs, amusement parks, and on local television talk shows. While I traveled with the group, we appeared on the *Dinah Shore Show* and flew to New York to do a guest appearance on a show called *Musical Chairs*. Occasionally, we even toured out of the country. I went to Japan with our group to make an album sponsored by Coca-Cola.

I found out early on that life on the road wasn't glamorous. It was hard work preparing and performing each night. We traveled from town to town by bus and plane, and while I saw many beautiful cities in the United States, soon all the towns began to look alike. Once we did a fourteen-week tour of one-night performances, traveling all the way from Florida to Maine by bus. Living on a bus can make you grumpy and irritable, and you have to find creative ways to relax. I had to pace myself and try to get as much sleep as possible. On traveling day, sometimes we had only a few hours to get ready for the show after we arrived in town.

As I adapted to my new life, my tears dried up, and I began enjoying the experience. I had to slap myself because I couldn't believe that I was in the group and traveling with talented performers, all with beautiful voices. Having such great coworkers helped make the transition easier. As time went on, Karen, Wendy, and I became like sisters, and there was never any rivalry among us.

I began to receive some wonderful reviews in local newspapers from the cities where we performed. The articles said that being the youngest member in the group wasn't an indication of my range of talent. They acknowledged me as a strong and versatile singer. One critic in Phoenix, Arizona, said, "I'm sure we will be hearing more from Lolita in the future." It breaks my heart today when I think of how I didn't let those reviews sink into my heart or allow myself to believe that eventually I could have made it as a solo entertainer.

Once my life started to fall into place, I became discontented. A deep longing to be married surfaced. I hadn't felt that compulsion before the tour; I had just wanted to sing and pursue my career. Now that my prayers were being answered, all I could think about was how lonely I was. I wanted to go home and climb into someone's nest.

99

Early in my life, two opposing dynamics had worked simultaneously in the lives of the people I loved. Now I was on my way to repeating the same destructive pattern. When I started traveling, the two opposing aspects of my personality began warring. There was the adult part of me that wanted to follow Christ and live a godly, productive life. Then there was the lost little girl starving for love and affection. She was tired of taking care of everyone else and wanted to find someone who would take care of her. Sad to say, the little girl was stronger, and she would do anything, no matter how irresponsible and reckless, to get her needs met.

I didn't understand why in the midst of my new success, I still felt sad and empty inside. Even though I never became a major celebrity, I can relate to movie stars and famous people who say that fame and fortune don't eliminate problems.

There's a high excitement that comes from the accolades of a cheering audience while you're performing on stage, but after the show is over, you stare reality in the face once again. When money and recognition didn't ease my loneliness, I once again decided that having a husband and children was the solution. I was still looking for something outside of myself besides God to solve my problems.

Many Christians view their conversion as a once-for-all experience that sharply divided their lives into what they were before it and what they were after. Their testimonies tell of how they walked down all the wrong paths until they accepted the Savior, at which point they experienced a dramatic transformation and began to live victoriously. Who wouldn't rejoice for brothers and sisters for whom this is true? However, this isn't the experience of all Christians. There are hosts of discouraged and often misunderstood believers who find the process of sanctification more like a spiritual roller-coaster ride as they learn to love, trust, and obey the Lord. I was one of those Christians.

I was, as the expression goes, "a person with just enough religion to be dangerous." I wore my cross whenever I performed, and I shared the gospel with many people while touring. I led others to the Lord, but I had no strong foundation in Christ myself. I was a baby Christian who had no clue about how to live for Christ. I was running the show, not God. I didn't know that responsibility came with the territory of professing to be a believer, and I was slow to learn that if you witnessed for Christ, your life needed to be surrendered to Him.

On tour, I occasionally drank in nightclubs and dated

nonbelievers I met while traveling. When I wasn't carousing, I was peering through the phone book looking for a church to attend. I stayed in my Bible and tried to get close to the Lord, but I didn't understand the forces warring inside me. I was a pitiful witness.

I eventually dated one of my coworkers. I liked him, but I wouldn't allow him to get too close. He made a crucial mistake; he began to care too deeply for me. His attention felt stifling. I didn't believe he really loved me, no matter how hard he tried to show me that he did. He wanted to marry me when he left the tour, but I ran from the relationship. He loved me, but I didn't love me. Rejection and abandonment felt more normal, and I subconsciously sought individuals who would grant me my sick wishes.

I preferred to fall in love with alcoholics or rebels. I felt more comfortable playing my old self-destructive childhood games with grown men. I seduced individuals who truly wanted to know me as a person because I thought that was the way I could stay in control. I had no idea I was participating in my own exploitation. Like most victims of sexual abuse, I felt like garbage and expected to be treated as such.

A highlight of my travels with the Christies came when we went to Chicago and my family saw me perform. They had always been very supportive of my singing, and they invited the entire group to my grandfather's house for a barbecue. My grandfather kept a scrapbook of all my reviews, so the band gave him an autographed picture and a copy of the album we had cut in Japan. He was so proud.

I also evangelized my family on that visit. Some family members gave their hearts to Christ. I told them how much Christ had done in my life, but I wasn't yet fully aware of how much work He still had to do before I was in any position to preach to anyone.

One day on tour I saw a magazine cover of Diana Ross and her beautiful family. She had a handsome husband and two adorable little girls. I had been invited to a party at her house when I was in high school, and I knew her younger brother Chico. I idolized Diana and was disappointed that she didn't receive an academy award for her magnificent performance in *Lady Sings the Blues*. I knew every song in that movie.

As I stared at Diana's family picture, I grieved my empty life. I didn't take into consideration that Diana had worked very hard to have both a career and a family. I was just beginning and didn't give myself a chance to pursue the career I truly wanted. I was delusional.

After a year on the road, I sent word to Sid that I wanted someone to take my spot, and he found a beautiful, talented young lady to replace me. I often wondered what might have happened in my career had I stayed with the New Christy Minstrels. I will never know, for in my search for the man of my dreams, I was about to begin a relationship that would change the course of my life forever.

As I was finishing my tour with the Christies, my estranged girlfriend Fran came back into my life. Eventually she received the Lord and was instrumental in helping my mother through her painful divorce proceedings. When I came home, we attended Bible study together and took tranquil drives to Malibu Beach. We drove up the coast late at night, sharing our hopes and dreams for the future and fantasizing about our future husbands and children.

On one of our drives, as we were marveling at the water shimmering in the moonlight, Fran caught me up on happenings at the Vineyard. My buddy John Smalley had married a good friend of ours named Dee Dee, and they were expecting twins. I was elated over the news. Our conversation eventually led us to a discussion about another friend in our fellowship. Fran told me that a new guy who was attending our church had really hurt our sister.

"JB has caused quite a stir in the church," she said. "A lot of girls like him. He shows up with some new girl each week."

103

The conversation shifted from JB to other bits of gossip. Then when we stopped at a red light, Fran got all excited.

"Look!" she exclaimed. She pointed to a huge billboard overlooking the strip. I saw a ruggedly handsome man posing in a green shirt for a Salem cigarette advertisement.

"Yeah?" I asked, not knowing why we were gazing at that particular billboard.

"There's the guy I told you about. That's JB. He's a model." I stared at the billboard until the light turned green and we drove away. He was older than I had expected. I thought he was nice looking, and there was something captivating about his smile. I was silent for a moment, and then for some insane reason, I said, "The Lord just told me he's going to be my husband."

She looked at me as though I had opened the chicken coop and let the birdies out.

"What?" she said. "You've got to be kidding."

I sat there smug and assured. "Nope. He's the one."

"Good luck. It would have to be God to get JB to settle down."

We continued riding around and talking, but my mind was on the man on the billboard. I didn't know one thing about him, and he didn't know one thing about the crazy woman claiming to be his future wife.

When I got home that night, I told my mother my ridiculous prophecy.

"The Lord didn't tell you that," she said.

My mother knew JB somewhat from church. She told me that he was friendly and outgoing but that he had a lot of problems. She was very troubled by my insistence that God had spoken such nonsense to me, and she did her best to convince me of my error.

Nothing my mother said about JB made any difference to me. My mind was made up. You see, I wasn't living on the same planet as everyone else. They lived on Earth; I lived on Neptune. Anything and everything was possible in my crazy world.

Warnings lights were flashing before I ever laid eyes on JB. Everyone I knew told me that he traveled in packs of females and that he was a drifter and a nonconformist. But I was bent on self-destruction, and in my insanity, I forged ahead. I figured it was the Lord's job to whip this man into shape for marriage—never mind the ton of work He had yet to do in my life.

Chapter Nine

THE MAN OF MY NIGHTMARES

One Sunday morning someone introduced me to JB at church. The billboard hadn't conveyed how stunningly handsome he was. He was what I imagined King David would have looked like. He was charming and charismatic, and he drew attention wherever he went. He and I connected immediately. Why wouldn't we? He was a seducer; I wanted to be seduced.

The following week, JB invited me to a concert at the church. When I arrived, I saw him across the street talking to a young girl. She was crying. Suddenly, she walked away, got in her car, and drove off. Watching the scene, I felt a knot in my stomach. It was clear that he had gotten rid of her, but I dismissed the obvious conclusion that whatever he did to her he would also do to me.

I plowed right through every stop, detour, and danger

sign that God posted in my path. JB and I hung out quite a bit after that first date. He was thirty-four years old, fourteen years my senior. He told me that he was divorced and had a twelve-year-old son, but I was emotionally detached from this vital information. Although deep in my gut I knew something was wrong, I told myself that I loved him and that God had put us together.

JB was a perfect composite of the men I had interacted with as a child. He gravitated toward broken women because they were easy prey and easy to dominate. He even discussed marriage on our second date and talked about how our children would look. It didn't seem inappropriate to me that our relationship was flying forward at the speed of light, but it appalled my mother.

"He's close to my age," she protested.

It didn't matter. No one and nothing was going to keep us apart. As a child, I had had people I loved yanked out of my life, and now that I was grown, I wasn't going to tolerate that kind of separation and agony again. I dug in my claws and fought to keep JB in my life.

By that time, I was addicted. And as in any addiction, I had to overcome my natural resistance to the unpleasant aspects of the relationship to stay hooked. After all, a taste for cigarettes and alcohol doesn't come naturally, and dope addicts need to be willing to endure bad drug trips. I bypassed all my painful emotional triggers and kept dating him, even though I was not happy in the relationship.

JB was as crazy making and confusing to me as my earlier role models. At times he was distant and neglectful; at others he was loving and protective. I got my fill of abandonment because he left town all the time without any notice. He'd be gone for six weeks or longer, and then one day show up at church as if nothing had happened. We'd resume our relationship right where we left off. He told me that on some of his trips, he went to live with Indians on a reservation. Other times, he spent time with his son.

I suffered depression not knowing when he was coming back. My heart soared whenever I drove into the church parking lot and saw his brown VW bus. After one trip, he finally gave me his address and invited me to visit him. I drove to a beautiful home on top of a hill overlooking the city.

I almost lost my teeth when I walked into the house. People were walking around naked and smoking weed. They were friendly and invited me to join in the skinny-dipping.

107

"No thanks," I said. "Where's JB?"

"He's in the back of the house," someone yelled out.

I bit my bottom lip, trying to keep from crying as I wandered through the madness until I found him.

"Is this your house?" I asked him.

"No," he said. "I'm staying with Inga."

"Inga?" I asked.

"She's a dear friend, that's all," he said. "Would I invite you up here otherwise?"

I started crying and ran back to my car. Inga may have been just a friend to JB, but he was driving her car and living in her house. I was sure she wouldn't have agreed with his description of their relationship.

JB was angry with me for leaving and didn't call me for a long time. I heard through others that he had left town again.

I was so depressed I could barely function. Eventually he sent me a letter telling that me he was in Colorado and asking me to join him. He told me that he had made living arrangements for me. He had also met a dear Jewish brother who sang, and he suggested that I work with the guy when I arrived. Mind you, he didn't send me any money. I used my savings to pay for all my travel arrangements. When I got my bus ticket, my mother hit the ceiling.

"Are you crazy?" she yelled. "You can't follow that man to Colorado. You don't know anyone there!"

As a true citizen of Neptune, details like that made no difference to me. JB's invitation was proof to me that God had spoken about our union. I truly believed that we were going to get married. I was convinced that while we were apart, JB had repented of his evil ways, and I was going no matter what. I had a need so deep that I believed only the promise of what I called love could fill it.

When I arrived in Glenwood Springs, I was elated to find JB waiting for me. He flashed me a dazzling, Tom Selleck smile and then hugged me and gave me a big kiss. We got my bags and headed for his car. All was well until we got there. An older woman was behind the wheel, and I stopped dead in my tracks.

"Who is she?" I asked.

"Oh, that's Lu. She's a dear friend, that's all. Would I invite you up here otherwise?" He introduced me to the woman driving the car. She looked uncomfortable, but she tried to be gracious to me.

They drove me to a hotel the first night because the people I would be staying with were out of town until the next day. That night JB and I were physically intimate for the first time. Before I left California, I had no intentions of having sex with him. Unfortunately, part of my out-of-control behavior was that sex never had anything to do with my choices. I went along because he expected me to, and I felt just as dissociated and violated as I had when my uncle molested me. The next day I felt dirty and cheap.

That evening, JB took me to meet the family I'd be staying with. He and Lu took me out to dinner before they dropped me off. It was a strange, uncomfortable meal. I'm positive he told her that I was just a friend, too, and I felt bad for both of us. I could see how happy she was sitting next to him and how much she cared for him. On my second day in Colorado, the lights finally came on: I should have never come. I had gotten myself in a mess, and I wanted to go back to LA.

Once again, the Lord was faithfully looking out for me. Before I even knew I was in serious trouble, God had provided a strong, loving Christian couple to help me. JB drove me to their home, where I would be living for a while. Ken and Carole had a precocious little daughter name Casey. She was the smartest two-year-old you could ever meet, and she had way more sense than I did. I soon fell in love with the entire family, and I began to confide in Carole. I told her how confused and unhappy I was with JB. I told both her and Ken what he told me about his relationship with Lu.

"That's a crock," Ken said. "He's dating Lu. We know both of them."

109

My heart sank. I felt convicted, and I confessed my sexual sin to Carole. She prayed with me while I sobbed. Then she said something that stunned me. "I hope you didn't get pregnant."

"That's impossible," I said through my tears. "It only happened once."

"No it isn't, honey," she said. "It only takes once."

I tried hard to make the best out of my situation in Colorado. I met Mike, the brother JB had spoken about. He was a guitar player and talented singer, and he and I and another girl started singing in local clubs. We mixed praise songs with our other numbers. The audiences enjoyed our music, and we had steady work. I made enough money to help contribute to Ken and Carole's household. I also went to church with my new adopted family and met wonderful brothers and sisters in their congregation. Everyone showed me love and affection.

I spent time with JB, too, but we didn't continue a physical relationship. He took me to Aspen a few times and to the mineral spas. We had fun together, but we never discussed anything deep or personal. I guess I was biding my time. Thanksgiving was approaching, and my mother and a close friend of hers were coming to visit me in Colorado for the four-day weekend.

By then I had missed my period and was feeling sick and tired all the time. Carole told me that I had to go to the doctor to see if I was pregnant. She let me wear her wedding rings to my appointment, and I used JB's last name. A couple of days later, I got a telephone call. "Congratulations, Mrs. Bills," a voice said, "you're going to have a baby."

I ran upstairs and closed myself in my room. For the first time since I had received Christ two years earlier, I truly repented before the Lord. I kept telling Him how sorry I was, and I begged Him to forgive me and help me. *I'm so sorry for not surrendering my life to you, Lord,* I cried. I was terrified. I had not only changed the entire course of my life, but I had also involved a totally innocent little life in my confusion. Neither JB nor I were responsible, stable individuals. I could barely take care of myself, let alone a child. It wasn't fair to my baby to have such unfit parents, but I had no one to blame but myself. I was staring my rebellion and stubbornness dead in the face.

I cried out to God to give me strength to go through the pregnancy and become a good mother. I never considered abortion. I wanted my baby and was determined to face my responsibility and take care of my child. How? I didn't know. I must have cried and prayed for more than two hours. After a while, I felt an incredible peace inside. I knew hard times lay ahead, but I felt a quiet assurance that God would see me through.

Later on, Carole hugged me, prayed with me, and told me she would help me tell my mother. Ken promised to talk to JB. He was furious with him because JB was much older than I was and never should have allowed something like this to happen. Their support was a blessing, but I was well aware of the old expression "it takes two to tango."

I combed Proverbs and Psalms looking for comfort. I had never really learned how to read the Bible. I just opened it and read what was in front of me. Nothing magical happened

111

when I began reading, but it was soothing to read King David's prayers and see how he felt when he sinned and disappointed the Lord. I went to bed that night a little closer to the Lord. I had taken one step closer to giving him more control in my life. Sad to say, there was still much more territory that He didn't occupy.

A day later, JB came over to take me out for a drive. Ken met him at the door and took him into the next room to talk with him. I didn't realize back then just how much God was with me. Even in the midst of my sin and disobedience, he provided me with a protective father figure to stand up for me. I was too ashamed to call Dad Hall and tell him of my predicament. Ari was no longer in my life, so I had no father to turn to. Ken provided a balance between discipline and unconditional love. He admonished me for my actions and told me that I had to start walking with the Lord and stop running my own show. Yet he still hugged me when I cried and told me that he understood. He assured me that God still loved me and would see me through my ordeal.

JB walked out of the den looking like someone had let all the air out of his balloon. Ken and Carole took Casey for a walk to give us some privacy. JB gave me a hug, and when he pulled me to his chest, I started crying. He was wearing a large metal cross. He took it off, put it over my head, and told me to keep it near my heart. I was happy because he always wore that cross, and it meant a lot to him. "Come on, let's get some coffee," he said. "We need to discuss the situation."

I was very relieved that he didn't seem to be angry with

THE MAN OF MY NIGHTMARES

me, but I felt like a five-year-old sitting across the table from her daddy. I knew I had been a bad girl, and I waited for his persona to change. I was sure any minute he'd start yelling horrible things at me. I was used to people in my life doing a Jekyll and Hyde switch on me.

Instead, JB began telling me about his childhood in Louisiana and what he termed his "unconventional" family. We had never discussed any of JB's personal life before. I sipped my coffee and listened. He told me about his distant, passive father and about his sister and his son. When he told me that his mother's sister used to have sex with him when he was a young boy, my eyes got big. "You're kidding," I said. He didn't answer me.

I figured if he could risk telling me something that awful, I'd open up and tell him about my past. I confided in him about how not only my uncle, but also a family friend had sexually assaulted me. I had never told anyone that before. He looked at me with compassion. "Honey, I can't tell you how common that is where I come from," he said. I was having a conversation with someone I had never met before that evening. He was vulnerable and exposed and sad, not seductive and playful as usual.

At the time, I didn't understand the full significance of what he was trying to tell me. I had no idea that our pasts had anything to do with our sickness and brokenness. I just thought we were swapping old war stories. Only God knew that one day I would need the information JB shared with me to help me cope and make peace with what had transpired between us.

That night I felt close and connected to JB. Unfortunately,

that was the closest he ever allowed me to get to him. His mood shifted abruptly. "Okay, enough," he said. "Let's talk about our baby. Don't worry. I'm going to take care of both of you. I promise. I'll be back for you tomorrow. I'm going to make arrangements to drive you back to LA. You need to be near your family now."

He told me that his mother was a prophetess and that he was going to talk over the situation with her. She would tell us what we should do and how we should take care of the baby. He also said hat he would deal with my mother because he knew she was going to hit the roof.

"Let's take it one day at a time," he said.

When JB dropped me off at Ken and Carole's, I felt much better. I told them about our conversation, and they were happy that he had taken the news so well and was willing to work out our situation together.

The next day, Carole and I were just returning from the store when I saw JB's van pulling away from the curb. When I walked in the house, Ken had a hurt expression on his face. I couldn't believe the story that unfolded. He told me that JB had come over to take back everything he had ever given me (which wasn't much). He had come for the cross, but I was wearing it, so he didn't get it.

"JB's mother told him that you were lying about it being his baby and to get away from you," Ken said. "She told him that you put roots out on him."

"Roots?" I asked. What on earth could she be talking about?

Ken said that according to JB's mother, black people in

114

the South were notorious for putting hexes and spells on their victims. She told JB that when she prayed, the Lord showed her that I was a liar who had put a hex on him.

I felt as if someone socked me in the stomach and drove a knife through my heart at the same time. My eyes filled with tears, and I could barely speak. In the past, I had never allowed myself to get really angry with people who mistreated me. I always made excuses for them and never felt hate toward anyone. Now I was filled with bitter rage at JB's mother. She had never laid eyes on me or spoken to me. How could she say something so vile and claim that it came from the Lord? She was from the South, not me. Putting hexes on others might have been a normal routine in her life, but it certainly wasn't a part of mine. How could JB believe that I would do something so evil to him?

115

As my anger turned to disgust, I thanked Ken for telling me what had happened. I believed that God had answered my prayer. I had already faced one huge obstacle, and at least I knew where I stood. A sense of inner calm and strength took over. My path was clear before me. I was determined to raise my baby alone. I was used to toughing out painful emotional crises. Very few people had ever held my hand and comforted me when I was terrified or distressed. I had to cope on my own, and I would cope again for the sake of my baby. I knew it wasn't going to be easy, but what had been easy in my life so far?

Chapter Ten

HEARING FROM GOD

JB left town. Rumor had it that he packed up and left everything behind, and I figured he was hiding out with the Indians. Frankly, I was relieved. I couldn't have handled the extra burden of knowing he was in town.

My mother was due to arrive in a couple of days, and my new church family rallied around me and prayed for her and me. I felt truly sad and remorseful. I hadn't purposely tried to hurt her. I had just been trying to fill the constant emptiness I felt inside. I didn't expect her to understand my irresponsibility. How could she? I didn't understand it myself. My mother was an intensely private person. For generations our family creed had been that what went on in our private lives stayed private. It wasn't going to be easy for her to face this situation publicly.

Carole and I met my mother and her friend Sara at the Greyhound bus terminal. When the bus pulled up, I was calm. God had given me enough time to come to terms with my situation. I was happy about my baby and had accepted that I would be a single unwed mother. After a cheerful greeting, we talked and laughed as we ate lunch.

Later on in the day, when my mother was settled in and relaxed, I took her aside and said, "Mom, I need to talk to you alone." She could tell by the expression on my face that it wasn't good news. She told me that she wanted Sara to be in on the conversation. Sara was her intercessory prayer partner.

Ken took Casey out for dinner, and we four women sat around the fireplace drinking hot tea. We prayed and asked the Lord to be in our midst.

"Mom, I'm having a baby," I said. "I am so sorry."

I didn't have to tell her who the father was. My mother lowered her head, and the color drained from her face. Her response was nothing like what I had expected. Although I could tell that it hurt her to the core, she remained quiet. She told me that she had known something was wrong.

"Yes," Sara said, "she knew something was up. That's why she asked me to come with her."

My mother was closer to me emotionally than I knew. She always had keen insight into my dilemmas. I believe she loved me in her way, but she didn't know how to reach out and show me. We both lacked the vital emotional limbs we needed to embrace each other.

I was relieved that God had prepared her heart, but it was still a painful time for both of us. We prayed and hugged each other and made an effort to enjoy the holiday despite the circumstances. The day before she returned to LA, she said to me, "I hope you are prepared for what you have to face. You've chosen a difficult path." I didn't answer her; we just held hands. After she left, I bought a bus ticket. I would return home the following week after I finished the singing engagements I had with Mike.

When it came time for me to leave, my heart broke. The night before, Ken and Carole's church congregation had a farewell dinner for me. My two singing partners were sad to see me go; we had made fine music together. People gave me gifts and cards. One brother gave me a lovely Star of David necklace and shared with me a verse the Lord had given him for me in prayer. It was in Psalm 121:1 "I lift my eyes to the hills—where does my help come from? My help comes from the LORD, the Maker of heaven and earth."

119

As the bus pulled out of the station that night, I had to stifle the sound of my sobbing by burying my face in my coat so I wouldn't disturb the other passengers. Fortunately, no one sat next to me until the next morning. Carole had prepared food for me to take on the bus and had put a lot of napkins in the bag. I went through napkin after napkin as I cried. I hadn't seen JB since that night at the diner, and I was devastated knowing that I was probably never going to see him again. All of the hopes and dreams I had when I left home to meet JB were now dashed. I put my hand on my abdomen and spoke to my baby. "I'm s-o-o sorry," I said. "What have I done to you? Now you won't know your father, either."

As the bus drove down that lonely black highway, my sorrow turned to dread when I thought about facing my brothers and sisters back home. Everyone had been so happy for me when I had left in October. Here it was the beginning of

December, and I was back already, an unwed mother. I thought about my family in Chicago. Not long ago, I had gone back there and evangelized everyone, and now I was pregnant. I loathed myself more than ever.

When I got home, things were strained between my mother and me. She never threw my situation in my face or said unkind things, but she was hurt and distant. She didn't know how to relate to me and didn't understand why I was so inconsistent in my walk with the Lord. Christ had made such a difference in her life, but it didn't appear that He was working in my life at all.

I was hanging on emotionally by a thin thread and needed to be alone for a while, so I decided to stay with Sara and her two young sons. Sara made a little space for me in one of her back rooms. My first night there, I woke up panicked and hyperventilating. I didn't know how to support my new family outside of singing, but a music career was now impossible. I knew my mother would help me, but she was still reeling from her divorce and wasn't in great shape financially.

It was after midnight, but I turned on the light and got out of bed. For some reason I felt led to open my Bible. I had done this many times during this ordeal, but so far nothing significant had happened. Still, I had a need to search the Scriptures for help. Crying, I again thumbed through the Bible looking for comfort. As I was turning to Proverbs, I somehow ended up in the book of Jeremiah. A passage jumped off the page and leaped into my heart:

"They are prophesying lies to you in my name. I have not sent them," declares the LORD. This is what the LORD says: "When seventy years are completed for Babylon, I will come to you and fulfill my gracious promise to bring you back to this place. For I know the plans I have for you," declares the LORD, "plans to prosper you and not to harm you, plans to give you hope and a future. Then you will call upon me and come and pray to me, and I will listen to you. You will seek me and find me when you seek me with all your heart." (29:9–13)

I fell to my knees and sobbed. God had spoken to me. My heart had been burdened and hurt by the awful prophecy JB's mother had spoken against my life, and God let me know that He had not spoken that profanity against me.

Even though I was relieved by the assurance that God had a plan for my baby and me, the passage made it clear that my deliverance from my circumstances wouldn't be swift. Even though Jeremiah was referring to the seventy years the Jews would spend in the Babylonian captivity, I knew that not following His ordinances had opened the way for the enemy to wreak havoc in my life for a long season.

It truly didn't matter at that point. I was just grateful that God had revealed Himself to me through Scripture. I had been taught that God speaks and confirms His will through the Word, and now I had proof that He had not abandoned me. I wiped the tears from my face, and from that night forward

I was no longer afraid. I had many challenges, sorrows, and hard times ahead, but I knew that the Lord was with me and that He would get me through.

A few weeks later, I moved back home and began to confront my situation head on. My church family, friends, mother, and little brothers rallied around and supported me. No one shunned me or made me feel like an outcast. People expressed their concern and lovingly exhorted me. Someone suggested that I counsel with a woman at Church on the Way in Van Nuys. This sister had a powerful restoration ministry. In addition to faithfully attending my home church, I had attended many services at the Church on the Way, and God had used Pastor Jack Hayford to introduce me to the concept of brokenness.

In the early seventies, I had heard Pastor Jack preach on Nehemiah 1:3: "They said to me, 'Those who survived the exile and are back in the province are in great trouble and disgrace. The wall of Jerusalem is broken down, and its gates have been burned with fire.'" Pastor Jack compared Jerusalem's broken wall and burnt gates to the condition of some believers in the body of Christ. He said that many people's emotional walls had been ravaged by the evil one and that God wanted to repair and restore them. That was the first time I had ever heard anyone preach about emotional problems. The sermon had fascinated me, but at the time I didn't see myself as one of the people whose walls were broken.

Nevertheless, I made an appointment to see the woman recommended to me at Church on the Way. I knew a few other brothers and sisters who had benefited from her ministry, and I figured I had nothing to lose. I was told that God had delivered her from oppressive depression and restored her.

The day I walked into her office, I felt numb and disconnected from my feelings. She greeted me graciously and then sat behind her desk observing me. I rattled off the story of my life as if I were talking about a trip to Disneyland. When I finished, she got up from her desk, came over to me, and laid hands on me. "Lord, please touch my dear sister and prepare her heart," she prayed. Then she sat down again and, after praying for other general areas concerning me, she looked me straight in the eye and said, "It's not time yet. The Lord showed me a picture of Lazarus in his grave clothes. You are bound in grave clothing."

123

I just stared at her. I had no idea what she was talking about. She went on to say that God would one day remove, strand by the strand, the bonds of oppression that shackled my life, but that I wasn't ready yet. She said that when He did the work, I would be like a person seeing sunshine for the first time.

I thanked her and left her office, disappointed and bewildered because I had expected more. I had heard what she had told others who went to see her, and I guess I was expecting her to give me a magic answer to all of my problems. However, I never forgot what she said to me, or the sermon Pastor Jack had preached on Nehemiah. I stored the information and went on with my life.

Being pregnant was a strange adjustment. One day I was full of faith; the next day I was depressed, missing JB. I didn't have a job or insurance, and I had to make arrangements to take care of my baby. So I went down to the county office and applied for welfare. It was the most humiliating experience of my life. Just months earlier I had been traveling to exotic places and making a lot of money singing; now I was standing in line at the welfare office. I wanted to cry as I filled out the forms. Eventually I received some money to live on, medical coverage for both me and the baby, and food stamps.

The county gave me physical provisions, but it was the Lord who supported me emotionally by speaking to me through Scripture. One night while I was praying, He led me to Isaiah 54:4–7:

> "Do not be afraid; you will not suffer shame. Do not fear disgrace; you will not be humiliated. For you will forget the shame of your youth and remember no more the reproach of your widowhood. For your Maker is your husband—the LORD Almighty is his name—the Holy one of Israel is your Redeemer; he is called the God of all the earth. The LORD will call you back as if you were a wife deserted and distressed in spirit—a wife, who married young, only to be rejected," says your God. "For a brief moment I abandoned you, but with deep compassion I will bring you back."

Once again I hit my knees in tears and gratitude. God never excused my behavior, but He let me know that He would restore me. I held that Scripture close to my heart as I went through my pregnancy. The Lord was my husband, and I was determined to walk uprightly with Him and raise my child to love and know Him.

The Lord also began to speak to me another way. Psalm 16:7 says, "I will praise the LORD, who counsels me; even at night my heart instructs me." That's what the Lord began to do for me. In my fourth month of pregnancy, I had a dream unlike any I had ever had before. I dreamed that I was having a conversation with the Lord. I couldn't see Him, but He told me who He was. He told me that the child I was carrying was a little boy and that He wanted me to name him Joseph. I told the Lord in the dream that I was grateful for a son and would love him, but that I had always thought that I would have daughters. "No," He said, "the child is a boy. Name him Joseph."

I woke up stunned. When I told my mother about the dream she said, "Joseph? We don't know anyone by that name. I don't think you could make something up like that. You need to obey the Lord then."

From that moment on, I told everyone that I was having a boy and not to buy me anything for a girl. I went to the Christian bookstore and bought a plaque with the name Joseph written on it in bold black letters. Joseph means "He shall add."

God spoke to me about most of the situations in my life, but never about anything pertaining to JB. I prayed that He would turn JB's heart around and bring him back into our lives, but God remained silent.

125

Chapter Eleven

SET FREE

As I awaited the birth of my son, I started going to a Saturday morning prayer group with my mother and her friends. Those times were part of God's plan to mend me. The women I called sisters were both a support group and powerful prayer warriors who taught me the value of intercessory prayer.

All these women were facing some seemingly insurmountable challenge or painful transition in their lives. Some were mothers grieving over children who had gone astray; others were praying for an unsaved husband, an unfaithful spouse, or a husband who had left them for a younger woman and with no means of support. Seeing how the enemy destroyed so many lives was overwhelming at times. We prayed that God would give each woman direction as she started her life over again. God used these women to provide support for me and three other pregnant women, two of whom were my age and also single. They prayed that JB and the other young men who had abandoned their unborn children would come back to take responsibility for their actions.

I learned two very important lessons in this prayer group. The first was the vital importance of having support from sisters in the body of Christ. Although I wouldn't really understand the importance of female support for years to come, the Lord was planting precious seeds for my future.

The second thing I learned was how to recognize and wage spiritual warfare. The Vineyard didn't teach much about the power of God or what it meant to stand against the enemy when he attacked. Our church was a perfect haven for battered souls to come in out of the storms of life and be cared for, but as we grew older in the Lord, there was a lot more we needed to learn about our spiritual journey. We needed to know about the pitfalls and dangers that lay ahead so we would be prepared for them. There were times when it was obvious that dark oppressive forces were at work in my life, and I had to learn to stand firm on God's promises in His Word.

I had not heard from JB, and I still felt abandoned and sad. My choices had cut me off from the natural flow of life, and I felt as isolated as I had in childhood. There was peace between my mother and me, but the distance remained. We didn't talk about my circumstances. I kept my pain to myself, as I always had.

By my eight month I had moved into a new apartment and was becoming excited as my due date drew near. When I got news that JB was back in town, at first I thought my prayers had been answered, but he made no attempt to contact me. When my sisters gave me a baby shower, I tried to have a good time, though I was troubled by JB's lack of concern. I pushed through the pain, and the day was a success until a concerned friend took me aside to tell me something.

She searched for the right words. "There's something I think you should know," she said. "It's so hard for me to break the news, but someone has to speak up. JB is engaged to a real young friend of mine, and she doesn't know about you."

My legs just about buckled beneath me, and my jaw dropped. "You've got to be kidding," I said.

She looked at me tearfully. "I wish I were."

As graciously as I could, I thanked her for the information. As she told me more about the young girl, I felt sick to my stomach. In bits and pieces I learned that she was a very naive nineteen and that her family was from another country. Somehow I managed to hide my true feelings and act as if I were in control. I stuffed my feelings down deep inside and extended my heart to the unsuspecting girl. My friend wanted to bring her over so that she could see for herself that JB was about to be a father. I agreed.

129

Later that evening my friend brought Cathy to my home. When she saw me, she started to cry. She didn't want to believe that JB had lied to her. We both sat down. I was crushed, but I didn't let either woman know it. I already felt like an idiot, and I was humiliated beyond words. I was pregnant by someone who obviously had never cared about me. I took his rejection as the deepest proof of how detestable I really was. It never dawned on me that JB cared for no one.

I took Cathy under my wing and became her defender

and protector. She seemed so much younger than me. At twenty-two, I felt like an old hag compared to her. She was so devastated that she could scarcely talk, so I was strong for both of us. I did all I could to console her and assure her that everything was going to work out. I was whistling in the dark, for I needed someone who could reassure me.

As we continued talking, Cathy asked me about my relationship with JB. I fed her the denial I had perfected over the years. I said that he had been kind and supportive of me until I got pregnant. Her eyes widened in disbelief. She said that she was afraid to cross him because he had threatened her with violence if she didn't do what he wanted. Now *my* eyes widened in disbelief. She asked me if he had ever hit me or threatened to do so. No, I told her—never! JB had always been even tempered. We couldn't help but wonder if he had multiple personalities.

I held up through the conversation, but when Cathy left, I sobbed. I was afraid to go to church next day. I had a strong feeling that JB would show up, and I didn't want to face him and Cathy in front of all my friends. I was sure the news of his engagement was going around the church. I wept and prayed, and as I read the Bible, the Lord led me to 2 Chronicles 20:17: "You will not have to fight this battle. Take up your positions; stand firm and see the deliverance the LORD will give you, O Judah and Jerusalem. Do not be afraid; do not be discouraged. Go out to face them tomorrow, and the LORD will be with you.'"

Once again, the Lord filled me with His incredible love and peace in a time of pain, and I got up the next day prepared to face the day. I was waddling up the steps to the church when I heard a familiar smooth southern drawl behind me. "Hey, sugar." My heart started pounding in my chest. I hadn't heard that voice in eight months. I turned around and there stood JB, alone. There was no one else around us. It was as though the Lord cleared the path and protected me.

JB walked up to me, put his hand on my stomach, and chuckled. "Man, you look like you're carrying a basketball," he said. His behavior was matter-of-fact, as if he had seen me just yesterday. He pulled me close to him and gave me a hug. "I've been praying for you," he said.

My mind was racing. *My God, I thought. He's engaged to someone else, and here he is hugging me and talking to me like a long-lost buddy.*

He went on talking in generalities, but I wasn't paying any attention to what he said. Occasionally, I saw twinges of compassion and conflict in his eyes. He kept reaching out to hug me, but then he'd pull away and talk about something meaningless. I was civil, but I didn't feel close to him, and I didn't want to say anything about the baby. He told me that he would be there for the delivery. I didn't care by that time; nor did I believe him. God was faithful. There was no scene, and I didn't feel embarrassed or humiliated. JB sat with me in church and then walked me to my car.

The next Saturday at prayer meeting, I shared my news about JB and Cathy. The group prayed on behalf of the baby and me, but one dear sister said to me, "We've been praying that God would give you an answer, and I believe He has. If God is closing the door, believe me, He is doing you a great favor." Deep down I knew she was right, but it still hurt.

I got up to use the bathroom, and as soon as I walked inside, my water broke. "I think I'm getting ready to have my baby!" I cried out.

At 11:30 PM, just half an hour short of the Fourth of July in 1977, Joseph was born. I was elated when I held him for the first time. Even though I never doubted that the Lord had spoken to me regarding his birth, it was a relief when the vision proved true. It was still so hard for me to believe that God would reveal Himself to me in such a profound manner. I gave Joseph his father's last name. Even if JB wasn't going to be in his life or take responsibility for him, I didn't want Joseph to grow up wondering who his father was.

132

I bumbled my way through the first couple of weeks. My mother helped me as much as she could, but she was still adjusting to her life as a divorcée and caring for my younger brothers. She had been forced into the working world, so she had a lot on her plate. My sisters in the Lord worked and had families of their own. When people could help me, they did. But for the most part I had to take care of Joseph by myself.

I wasn't prepared for all the drastic changes. I assumed that the baby was there to keep me company. Wrong! I was there to take care of his needs, not the other way around. My first course in reality 101 was the awareness that a good mother laid down her own aspirations for the sake of her baby. I would have plenty of time to figure that one out. I also had the crazy notion that Joseph would fit in my plans where I had left off nine months earlier. Wrong again. I was no longer free to roam about the country and do as I pleased. Joseph was now my number one priority.

Changing diapers and giving the baby baths were the least of my problems. I had taken care of small children since I was seven. The hardest part was the loneliness and lack of freedom. Joseph nursed every two hours, and I couldn't leave him for long periods of time. In the wee hours of the morning I felt there was no one else in the world, and at times the loneliness was overwhelming. As the reality of my situation kicked into full gear, I was full of rage at JB for abandoning me, but I had no way of processing my feelings. I had to rely on the survival skills I had adopted in my childhood, so I stuffed my anger.

Then one day JB came over unexpectedly. I felt about as close to him as I would have to the milkman. I invited him in, but I felt cold and kept my emotional distance. I guess in his broken way, he was trying to reach out to Joseph. I do have one precious memory of his visit. He took Joe out of his crib, hugged him, and said, "He does look like me." I had done nothing to convince him that Joseph was his child. I had made up my mind that I wasn't going to try to force him to be in our lives. Maybe my determination to take care of my son with or without his help made him realize that I wasn't a voodoo queen.

JB came over one other time, bringing a female hitchhiker with him. She looked shattered and lost. I just shook my head; the leopard hadn't changed his spots.

One day my pastor called me and asked me to come to his office for a meeting. Pastors of other churches had called him

133

about JB's relationships with women in their congregations, and he had heard the rumors circulating in his own church. I didn't want to go because I was afraid he was going to call me on the carpet, but I went just the same. When I got to the meeting, I was stunned to see Cathy and Lu. We timidly took turns telling the pastor our stories.

The details were more sordid than any of us had imagined, and it was sickening coming to terms with the fact that JB had betrayed so many. When the whole story finally came out, nine different women were involved (ten, really, but no one knew about Inga but me). One of the women who came forth was the young girl I had seen crying at the concert. I later found out that she had tried to commit suicide because of JB.

Our pastor told us that JB was coming to his office in a few days and that he was going to confront him about his actions. I knew how rebellious JB was in terms of submitting to authority. He had told me on many occasions that he was only interested in what Jesus had to say and that he read only the red print in the Bible. He didn't consider Paul or anyone else in Scripture an authority he needed to obey. He said they were mere men, just like he was. *Good luck, Pastor,* I said to myself.

After the meeting, Cathy told me that she was no longer engaged to JB. Her father had finally put his foot down and run him off the property. Lu told me that when she saw me wearing JB's cross, it tore her heart. "That was my cross," she said. "I gave it to him as gift." My heart went out to Lu, for she had been with JB for years. Cathy and I were young and hopeful about the future, but Lu was close to JB's age and had much more of an investment in him. I don't think she had an easy time moving on. Later, I gave her back her cross. It hadn't been JB's to give.

Feeling broken and used, we fell silent as we tried to make sense of what we had just heard. There were no words for the pain we each bore. I thought about my innocent baby, who had nothing to do with his father's pathology. What kind of heritage had I given him?

The pastor asked me to come to his meeting with JB. He wanted to know what his plans were regarding the baby and me. I was afraid of what JB would think when he saw me there. I feared he would blame me and think I had called the meeting. I was the one with reason to be angry, but I never allowed myself to feel the extent of my rage toward him. I was far more concerned about JB's welfare than my own. However, I wasn't about to disobey my pastor.

A few nights before the meeting, God gave me a vivid dream about the situation. I saw a man in a pickup bound by many chains. There were other men sitting next to him, escorting him to a meeting. I saw that the men's heads were not protected with helmets, and I knew that in order for them to deal with this man, they would have to protect their minds. The bound man was clever and would play games with them. The message was clear: If the men were not equipped with God's Word, the meeting would not be successful.

I got to the meeting early and found our pastor with the other four pastors whose churches JB's womanizing had affected. They had all come to confront him. I told them about the dream God had given me and said they would have to protect their minds from the games JB would play.

135

I was surprised that JB showed up, but he did. He looked agitated as he walked past me. Before they questioned him about the other accusations, they asked him what his intentions were regarding our son. JB looked over at me, his eyes wide with fear. He looked like a first-grader who had been called to the principal's office. He said he wanted to call his mother, and he called her right there in the pastor's office. Somewhere in the conversation, she asked to speak to me. I looked at him as if he was crazy. Why would I want to talk to his mother? I got on the phone anyway. A chill went through my body at the sound of her voice.

There was no warmth or tenderness in it, but she had the presence of mind to watch what she said. Her son was in deep trouble, and I was surrounded by men of God that the Lord had raised up to come to the defense of the women her son had mistreated. She got right to the point.

"If you get a blood test for Joseph," she said, "we'll take it from there." *For what?* I thought. For one thing, I wasn't going to subject my baby to a blood test in order for her to accept him, and for another, testing might give her legal power over him. I quickly handed the phone to JB. I wanted no part of her, and I wasn't about to have Joseph tested.

After JB told the pastors he would take care of Joseph, they asked me to step into the other room. I sat outside the door, shaking. They kept him in there for more than an hour. Then all of a sudden, JB threw the door open and ran past me. I followed him, trying to ask him what had happened. He turned around, gave me a look filled with hate and contempt, and headed out of the building.

I went back to the pastor's office. My dream was pretty close to what had transpired. My pastor said that JB wouldn't repent. When they tried to pray over him, he objected and finally ran out. My pastor called every church in the area and told them to contact as many churches as possible to warn them that JB was unrepentant and a danger to the body of Christ.

The truth had come out, and as painful as it was, it had set me free. I never saw JB again.

Chapter Twelve

ON THE ROAD AGAIN

y first year as a mother had many challenges, but many rewards, too. Taking care of Joseph got easier as I began to feel better physically and could take him out of the house for visits. Joseph brought joy and healing to our family. My mother and his two young uncles fell in love with him. The distance between my mother and me lessened for a while, as we now had a common bond in caring for Joe. Joseph had no relationship with his father's side of the family, Ari didn't know about him yet, and the rest of our family was in Chicago, so our spiritual community became his extended family, and God gave him uncles, aunties, and cousins.

To keep busy, I got involved in the gospel musicals that the Vineyard began to put on. It proved to be a rich time. I got even closer to my brothers and sisters, and Joseph became the Vineyard baby. Everyone took turns watching him while I did my scenes. I didn't feel lonely during that time. With rehearsals, dinners, prayer group, and fellowship, I was busy and happy.

Unfortunately, like all good runs, the show eventually came to an end, and once again I was faced with myself. After I got pregnant, I was determined not to get involved with any more men until the Lord sent me a husband. I had Joseph dedicated to the Lord, and I walked upright before God…for a while. My willpower sustained me for a short time, but then I began acting out again.

I began dating the nephew of the friend whose apartment I was renting. I started out with the good intention of ministering to him and bringing him to the Lord, but it didn't end up that way. Had I been able to see the relationship for what it was supposed to be, he would have been a great friend. He was nice and a lot of fun. We saw each other for a few months, and then my period was late again. Joseph was only thirteen months old.

I cried hysterically. *What is the matter with you?* I asked myself over and over. Obviously, something was terribly wrong with me, but what? How could I have gotten myself in this situation again, and so soon? I hit my knees and again begged the Lord for forgiveness.

I hadn't even considered having an abortion when I became pregnant with Joseph, but now when I thought I was pregnant, I was determined not to have the baby. There was no way I could go through that again, and I couldn't put my family and church through it again, either. My decision to have an abortion if I were pregnant troubled me for years to come. I never thought I would contemplate that action, even though Mama

140

Hall had often told me, "Never say what you won't do. Given the right set of circumstances, we're all capable of anything."

She was right. While I don't by any means condone abortion, I can certainly understand the desperation and fear that would lead a woman down that path. Once an unwed woman is pregnant, more heartbreak and sadness are the results, whichever path she chooses. The fact that I didn't end up pregnant or having an abortion didn't change the fact that I was living in sin—and sin has consequences.

I hadn't taken into consideration that I had been nursing and that my menstrual cycle was not back on track yet. Not long afterward, my cycle resumed. I cried and thanked the Lord profusely. That situation scared me terribly. I went the next four years without getting involved with anyone else. I learned my lesson...for a while.

I sought God's forgiveness and intervention in my unruly life, and to keep from acting out again, I closed down emotionally and put myself in isolation. My life was always either black or white. There was never any in-between. My dating life consisted of allowing myself to be sexually exploited or being all alone. Trying to stop my inappropriate behavior was like dieting. The harder I tried to stop, the more I wanted it. I never dated as friends and thus denied myself healthy, non-sexual encounters with good men.

I had other challenges to face when my family back in Chicago found out I had a baby. I hurt one cousin in particular. When I had gone back to Chicago earlier, I had led her to the Lord and encouraged her to read the Bible. I told many family members about Jesus. I don't think anyone would have thrown stones at me had I leveled with them. Instead, I had run and hidden, leaving a trail of messes.

Ari also found out about Joseph. He was very quiet when he met him. I don't think he knew what to say. He was always gracious and kind to Joseph and embraced him warmly as his new grandson, but he surely must have wondered why all the effort he had expended on me appeared to have been in vain.

I was content taking care of Joseph, but I looked for a job because I didn't want to stay on welfare and food stamps. The father of my former boyfriend William was an optometrist, and he offered me a position as a receptionist. I worked for him for more than a year. It wasn't easy going to work and taking care of a toddler. I had to find a babysitter for Joseph, and day care was very expensive. Leaving him was hard on both of us. He cried when I had to leave, and I felt guilty the entire day.

On many a day I thought about the opportunities I had forfeited with the Christy Minstrels and how I had complicated every area of my life. At those times I really resented JB. He was free to live his life in the same irresponsible and selfish way he always had. All the pressure of parenting fell on my shoulders. I had no choice but to do exactly what countless other single mothers like me had to do: I put one foot in front of the other and did what was necessary to take care of Joseph and me.

I happened to run into two friends from my high school days who were single moms, too. They both had children the same age as Joseph. Having friends made life bearable. Joseph had buddies his age to play with, and we girls had the support and comfort of one another. Occasionally a dear brother from church took me out to dinner and a movie. Though I didn't recognize it then, I was starting to make healthy male friend-ships. My brothers treated me with the utmost respect and kindness, and I was too steeped in self-destruction to ever have considered one of them as a romantic interest. I didn't feel deserving of their love, and I wouldn't allow myself to get too emotionally attached.

One of my most precious memories is of the Friday night spaghetti dinners at the home of four roommates who attended the Vineyard. After the concerts, the guys opened their home to anyone who wanted to fellowship. As soon as you walked in the front door, you heard Keith Green or another popular Christian artist playing on the stereo. Some people were laugh-ing and talking as they prepared food in the kitchen; others were lounging in the living room playing board games or just visiting. The guys rallied around Joseph when I came over. They took him outdoors and played with him. God sur-rounded Joe and me with a loving group of people to help us.

143

I met wonderful people from all walks of life at those Friday night gatherings. I think sometimes believers miss out on opportunities to just visit and get to know one another. So many gatherings revolve around Bible study or prayer time. Those are good things, but I also think it's important for people to have a place to go and sit down and laugh and share in the Lord for fun and recreation. I believe Jill would have been pleased with those Friday night dinners. They were like the people centers she dreamed about.

At the same time I was working as a receptionist, I began to attend the Vineyard School of Ministry in order to learn more about the Word of God, grow stronger in my faith, and get closer to the Lord. God had a wonderful blessing in store for me there. Two people in my class, Debby Boone and her boyfriend, Gabriel Ferrer, were to have a big impact on my life.

Debby was a beautiful, vivacious young woman. Her parents, Pat and Shirley Boone, were a musically talented, dynamic couple who loved the Lord. Gabriel was warm, personable, and funny. His parents were the late actor José Ferrer and singer Rosemary Clooney, a close friend of my mother's. Debby was friendly to me, but I was closer to Gabriel's family from the early Vineyard days. His sisters, Maria and Monsita, and Monsita's husband, Terry, were my prayer partners and were very close to me during my ordeal with JB. Gabriel's two brothers, Raphael and Miguel, were dear to my heart.

At the time I began attending Bible studies at the Boone home, Debby's singing career was about to take off, and her parents asked us to pray for her future. Next thing we knew, she had the monster hit "You Light Up My Life." After she stepped out as a solo artist, word got to me that she was putting a band together to go on tour and that she would be opening in Atlantic City in a few weeks.

I believe that God spoke to me through Scripture regarding touring with her: "See, I have placed before you an open door that no one can shut" (Revelation 3:8). I felt He was telling me to audition, even though rumor had it that her managers already had someone else in mind to sing backup for her. I was nervous the day I went to the audition. There was a lot going on when I arrived, and there were people everywhere. I started to turn around and go home, but I felt

I had heard from the Lord, so I stayed and waited for my turn to sing.

Debby, her two managers, and her musical conductor, the late Don Costa, were holding the auditions. When Debby saw me walk into the room, she smiled and said, "I didn't know you sang."

I had chosen a song from a musical that was popular at the time. I don't remember the name of the show, but the song was "Thank Heaven for You." It was an up-tempo, in-your-face kind of a tune. I took a deep breath and gave it all I had. The group seemed pleased, but you never can tell about auditions. They told me that whatever the outcome, they would contact me later. I went home and sat by the telephone for the rest of the day and into the evening.

By eight o'clock I was certain that they had hired the other singer, and I was upset because I felt that I hadn't heard from the Lord after all. At eleven, my mother told me to call Henry, the leader of Debby's band and a dear brother in the Lord. I said that it was too late to call his house and that he would have called me by now if I had gotten the job.

"You don't know that," my mother insisted. "Just call."

My hands were trembling, but I reached for the phone and called him. A sleepy Henry answered the phone. "Didn't anyone call you?" he asked in a surprised voice. "You got the job."

I began to cry out of sheer joy. Despite my many failures, God had blessed me again. When Henry told me how much money I would make on tour, I lifted my hands and praised the Lord. Now I could get off welfare.

Rehearsal soon began, and I got to see just how much

hard work went into preparing for a solo show. I had never thought it was that big a deal for an entertainer to sing for forty-five minutes or an hour on stage. It had never dawned on me how many songs it took to fill up even thirty minutes. There had been seven entertainers with the Christies, so it hadn't been nearly as demanding as one person carrying the whole show.

Debby's music arrangers gave us musical packets that they continued to revise as we learned the show. There was a lot of material to learn in three weeks. I felt sorry for Debby as she walked around with a headset and a little tape recorder, learning her material. She had to prove to many skeptics that she was a talented singer apart from her family. I had to learn the backup parts, but Debby had to learn new music and all the lyrics, too. I was glad the pressure wasn't on me.

Debby's life was the closest thing to a fairy tale I had ever seen, yet I can honestly say I never felt envious of her blessings. Her life was so far removed from mine that it would have been ridiculous to compare our lots in life. There was a purity and innocence and spontaneity in Debby's life that was not in mine. She was youthful and carefree. I had walked a lonely path and had experienced life way beyond my years.

While I was truly glad for Debby, there was one aspect of her life that made me sad—her relationship with her family, especially her father. Each night in the show, Debby would sing to a large screen of photos of herself as a little girl, her parents, and her sisters. She sang a beautiful sentimental song as a tribute to her father. I would sit quietly on my stool in the darkness while she performed that number and wipe the tears from my eyes as I watched two-year-old Debby sitting on her daddy's lap and kissing him.

I didn't realize that my tears were for the biological father and the sense of belonging I had never known. I often wondered what it would have been like to have the close father-daughter relationship that Debby had with Pat. I marveled how much she looked like him. There was no question about her lineage and where she came from. I wish that I had realized then that as I sat in the darkness surrounded by His presence, God was using Debby and Pat to show me how much He loved me.

I was happy and so thankful to be out of hot water, and I knew that God was working in my life. So far in my mending process, He had saved me, placed me a spiritual family, and given me a support network. He had removed JB from my life and given me revelations from Scripture and in dreams that guided me and assured me of His presence. Yet I still didn't realize how much He loved me, for I still did not love myself. I was like a broken jar of clay that couldn't hold what God poured into me, and I still felt empty and hollow inside.

PART III

A Broken Cistern

JARS OF CLAY

JOSEPH BYRD

What at first was just a pot
has shown it can hold a lot.
A simple jar that could be more,
Refiner's fire has turned to ore.

The Lord is good all the time,
He takes what's His and makes it mine.
People pass me day by day,
not knowing treasure's in this jar of clay.

On His table, I turned and turned,
just to be of value is all I yearned.
Though dust gathers as I sit on this shelf,
the Potter, inside, conceals my wealth.

Who can use him, that's what they say,
Not knowing treasure's in this jar of clay.
Jars of clay
Jars of clay

It doesn't matter what they say,
all that's gold don't glitter, but clay is clay.
What you see is what you get,
until you put your hand in the heart of it.

The Lord is good all the time,
He takes what's His and makes it mine.
People pass me day by day,
Not knowing treasure's in this jar of clay.

Chapter Thirteen

THIRSTING AT
THE WELL

There were no tears when I left on tour this time. I moved back home with my mother so she could take care of Joseph while I traveled. Whenever we were performing close to home, she, my younger brother Tufa, and Joseph would come stay with me.

I visited some spectacular places during the three years I toured with Debby, including Japan, Taipei, the Philippines, and China. One of the highlights was Debby's invitation to sing at President Reagan's inaugural ball in 1981. During rehearsals for our segment of the gala, I felt like a kid at an enormous festive birthday party. Scores of celebrities, singers, dancers, and comedians were present. As we walked through one of the grand ballrooms after Debby's performance, I passed Jacqueline Kennedy Onassis, a strikingly beautiful woman, small in stature but dynamic in presence. Patty Hearst was a few yards ahead of me talking to a crowd of reporters. When we got inside the van, all the band members swapped stories about the rich and famous they had encountered.

That night the snow lay white and crisp on the ground. Beautiful glittering lights decorated the Capitol building and the surrounding area. It was truly a winter postcard moment, and yet in the midst of all that beauty, I still felt disconnected and dead inside. These and other moments on tour were pleasurable, but fleeting. I wanted so much to enjoy them, but I always seemed to be looking through a dim window at a world that was off-limits to me. Even though I still felt sad inside, I was determined not be ungrateful to the Lord for providing this opportunity, and I fought hard not ruin it as I had with the Christies. Every day I put on a big smile and carried on.

When Don Costa stopped conducting for Debby, she rotated between two musical directors, Marty Goetz and Paul Johnson. Paul occasionally brought his pretty, vivacious wife on tour with us. Her name was Kathie Lee. Kathie was a kind-hearted, generous young woman on stage and off and a talented singer and performer, with a flair for musical comedy. I became close friends with both her and Paul. I spent a lot of time with her outside of work and frequently visited them at their home.

Kathie performed quite a bit in Reno, Nevada, opening for Shecky Greene. When she began getting more singing engagements, she asked me if I would sing background for her in between my gigs with Debby. I had to get Debby's permission because I was on a retainer. (Some performers pay their band members half their salaries not to go on tour with another band.) Debby was a new mother and had carefully rearranged her schedule. We had some time off, so she was all right with the idea. As life would have it, however, Paul and Kathie eventually went their separate ways. Kathie later married Frank Gifford and went on to have huge success on *Live with Regis and Kathie Lee*. To say the least, our lives went down different paths.

When I was singing for Debby, Las Vegas became like a second home to me. We often performed two shows a night at the Rivera Hotel. On occasion, Lola Falana, who was performing down the street at the Aladdin Hotel, rented a local skating rink after hours and invited all the performers from shows on the Strip to skate to the latest disco hits.

153

Debby and Gabriel skated, and once Robert Goulet came whisking by on his skates, laughing merrily. However, most of the other stars were probably too tired to boogie after their gigs, so the band members of the headliners were usually the ones at the parties. I got to know some of the band members of Kenny Rogers, Tony Orlando, Glen Campbell, and a host of others.

My mother was the toast of the town when she visited. She outskated us all. Back in Chicago, she had skated quite a bit as a teenager. It was fun to watch her skating backwards and waving to the beat of the music.

I met a stranger at one of those parties. He wasn't a musician, so I don't know how he got an invitation. There was immediate chemistry between us. After my last show he showed me the hip nightspots and took me for drives through the dark desert around Vegas. He was a gentleman and never harmed me in any way, but it was foolish on my part to be so trusting. His behavior was mysterious, and I never knew anything about him. For a young man, he carried around large sums of money. He would disappear for days, and then show up out of the blue, just as he did that night at the skating rink.

We never had an intimate relationship, but by my fierce emotional attachment to him troubled me. I knew something was terribly wrong with me because of the panic I felt whenever he had to leave. I didn't want him out of my sight, even though I kept telling myself, *You don't know this man.* I lost contact with him as time went on, but it took me a while to get over him.

Not long ago there was a story on television about how serial killer Ted Bundy lured his unsuspecting victims to their demise. The public cringed wondering how women could be so trusting, even though Bundy appeared as normal and safe as the guy next door. I think that need sometimes far outweighs common sense. I thought back to driving all over Vegas with a guy I barely knew, and I was truly grateful to the Lord that my body hadn't been found somewhere in a remote desert area.

One night in Las Vegas, I stared sadly at the glittering lights of the casinos from a luxurious suite on the top floor of the Aladdin Hotel. All the glamour in the world couldn't erase the deep emptiness and pain I felt all the time. My old longing resurfaced, and even though I went to great lengths to keep from acting as before, I barely escaped calamity again. I managed

154

to meet two guys who were emotionally unstable. One was an alcoholic, although he tried to get help. He visited me on the road whenever possible. We cared for each other, but it was a long-distance situation.

I was also having bouts of deep depression. I was fine as long as I was on tour traveling and doing things, but the minute our plane touched down back home, I'd panic. I wanted to see Joseph and be with him, but I felt like a lost little girl coming home to him. I was scared to face life without the structure of the band.

Ever since I was a little girl I had found safety in routine, and when I was on the road, I knew what was expected, just as I had earlier at school. My schedule was determined beforehand. At home, however, I was the structure for other people's lives. To deal with feeling out of control, I'd clean my room and put everything in order. After I unpacked, did my laundry, and got Joseph settled in for the night, I felt better.

Life at home was getting more difficult. My mother and I were both raw and in an emotional tailspin, and we argued all the time. She was devastated when Ari remarried; I felt stuck and trapped, wanting to find a mate and move on with my own life. We took out our anger and hostility on each other. I think both of us had expectations we wanted the other to fulfill. I felt that she interfered in my life, and I certainly wasn't the model daughter she had probably hoped for. I didn't have any of that awareness then, though. Everything was just confusing and chaotic. Although my mother hadn't resumed her drinking in full force, she was still battling it, and it was also causing problems.

As our arguments intensified, they upset Joseph, who by this time was three and going to preschool. "I tell my teacher," he would threaten. I felt so bad that he obviously felt insecure with both my mother and me. It was painful that our home was so volatile. Some of our arguing was escalating into physical assaults. Rage was everywhere. I still tried to get closer to the Lord, but I kept running into a brick wall. I struggled to feel close to Him. How come others weren't having such a hard time walking with God and trusting Him?

One evening I heard a sermon on television that distressed me. The text came from John 4:13–14. Jesus was talking to the Samaritan woman, and He said, "Everyone who drinks this water will be thirsty again, but whoever drinks the water I give him will never thirst. Indeed the water I give him will become in him a spring of water welling up to eternal life." After the sermon, I read more about the Woman at the Well. Jesus told her that she had had five husbands, but she was still not satisfied.

I identified with the Samaritan woman. I had not yet been married, but I was going from one romance to the next without taking a breath in between. My mother told me that I reminded her of my grandmother, who had been in love with love. Grandmother had said to her on more than one occasion that the best way to get over one relationship was to find another one, and now my mother saw me walking down that path. However, new romances never eased my pain or spared me from my worst nightmare of being alone. I never really knew if I truly cared for someone or if my affection was all about dependence.

I got on my knees and started crying. I just couldn't understand why I was still thirsting for more outside of God. I had accepted Christ in my heart, but I still felt empty and lonely all the time. I wanted the water Jesus promised the Samaritan woman. I wanted the eternal water of the Holy Spirit to spring up inside of me and fill me so I wouldn't be in such a state of need all the time. I pleaded with Him to fill me with so much of Him that I would never need another romantic relationship.

After my prayer, I got Joseph ready for bed and started to read the Bible. I sought comfort, and as always I began reading in Psalms and Proverbs. However, my eyes fell upon a passage in the Book of Isaiah:

> Give ear and hear my voice, listen and hear my words. Does the farmer plow continually to plant seed? Does he continually turn and harrow the ground? Does he not level its surface, and sow dill and scatter cummin and plant wheat in rows, barley in its place, and rye within its area? For his God instructs and teaches him properly. For dill is not threshed with a threshing sledge, nor is the cartwheel driven over cummin; but dill is beaten out with a rod, and cummin with a club. Grain for bread is crushed; indeed, he does not continue to thresh it forever because the wheel of his cart and his horses eventually damage it. He does not thresh it longer. This also comes from the LORD of hosts, who has made His counsel wonderful and His wisdom great. (28:23–29, NASB)

I walked over to the window and looked outside at the lights, pondering what I had just read. I had a sense that God was telling me that He was going to straighten out my life and make something beautiful out of my mistakes and heartaches. Yet I also felt that He was telling me that it would not be a quick, painless process and that I wouldn't understand the ways He would work in my life. That night I wrote beneath that Scripture, "Lolita, how you are planted will be determined by the Lord's wisdom, but the end results will be worth it."

This passage of Scripture gave me peace because it explained some of the pain I had already endured. I felt assured that the Lord had heard my prayers and that He was showing me that different kinds of crops required a different process in order to reap a harvest. He helped me understand that He had a unique plan for each person's life and that, just as my path in life was very different from the paths of Debby and Kathie Lee, so would be the ways He healed and restored me.

I thought I knew exactly what the Lord meant in that Scripture. Because I felt so bruised inside from the road I had already traveled, I truly believed that the scattering, crushing, threshing, plowing, sledging, and clubbing had already taken place. I was sure that God meant the worst was behind me. I had no idea that He was speaking about my future and confirming what the woman at Church on the Way had said about my emotional healing. The process Isaiah described was yet to come.

I had been praying steadfastly for a mate, and that same evening, God gave me another Scripture from Isaiah that gave me hope: "Seek from the book of the LORD, and read: not one

158

of these will be missing; none will lack its mate. For His mouth has commanded, and his Spirit has gathered them" (34:16, NASB). A month later, the Lord led me to yet another Scripture: "I will pour water on the thirsty land, and streams on the dry ground; I will pour out my Spirit on your offspring, and my blessing on your descendants. They will spring up like grass in a meadow, like poplar trees by flowing streams" (Isaiah 44:3–4). The next verse referred to two other sons.

So far, Joseph was my only offspring, and I thought for sure I would remain single and raise him alone. At twenty-five, I felt washed up. I closed my eyes and prayed, *God are You telling me that one day I'll have other children?* I felt so lonely and cut off from the rest of the world that I couldn't imagine ever finding love and having more children. Still, I marked those promises in my Bible and prayed for a miracle.

Chapter Fourteen

MARRY IN HASTE

On Thanksgiving Day, 1982, I was cranky and lethargic. My mother wasn't cooking the meal that year; instead, we were going over to my cousin Pat's house for dinner. I didn't want to go anywhere. If I had had my wish, I would have stayed at home and watched *The Twilight Zone* marathon that was playing all weekend. Still, I had to think about Joseph. It wasn't right to deprive him of the holiday because I was down.

My life was at a standstill; I was still touring, but not as much. Debby was starting to do live play performances and was preparing to take her show *Seven Brides for Seven Brothers* to Broadway. This meant she wasn't using the band as before, and I had nothing new to look forward to.

I loved my family, but I was tired of hanging out with just women. Since I believed that God had spoken to me through Scripture two years earlier about having a mate, I had been preparing Joseph for the day he would have a daddy. I think I primed him too well. At five, he went around telling people, "I'm getting a new daddy." I hadn't met anyone I was interested in, and after a while I figured I had misunderstood the Scripture.

I literally had to drag myself to celebrate Thanksgiving. I had no energy. Thankfully, my cousin made it a special evening for my family. She had decorated her dining room in warm earth tones and put scented candles on the table. The food was delicious. Eventually I relaxed and enjoyed myself, even though I still had a heavy heart. After dinner, I had a conversation with a nice young woman who had joined us for the evening. Her name was Barbara, and she was in a play called *Peaches* at the Ebony Showcase Theatre. In passing, she remarked, "The director is looking for an understudy for my part."

I hope he finds her, I thought.

"Hey," she said, "why don't *you* audition?"

"Me?" I said. "You have to be kidding. I'm no actress."

She said the role was for a beautiful woman who had emotional problems. I could certainly relate to the part about emotional problems, but I didn't consider myself beautiful. In fact, my low opinion of myself had cost me a possible modeling career. And now Barbara was trying to convince me to try out for the part of a beautiful vixen. She told me about the play and cast and how handsome, talented, and dedicated David, the leading man, was. He was a lot of fun, all the girls liked him, and he got excellent reviews.

After JB, I'd had my fill of handsome, funny men that all the girls liked, and I wasn't interested in auditioning. She didn't give up until I finally agreed to at least see the play. I went home that evening angry with myself for saying I'd go, but a few weeks later I went to see it.

I must admit that I was very impressed. Barbara played the leading female character, Peaches, who had been sexually abused as a child (ironic, huh?). The subject was handled tastefully, and the acting was superb. The scenes between Barbara and David were dynamite. After the play, I tried to slip out quietly while the actors were meeting their fans in the lobby, but my mother and her girlfriend insisted that we stay. They wanted to meet the cast.

I slowly moved closer to the front door, intending to wait outside, but Barbara saw me and came and got me. She took me over and introduced me to Kenny, the creator of *Peaches*. We shook hands. "This is Lolita, the girl I was telling you about," Barbara said.

I told him how much I enjoyed the play. He was warm and personable, and we talked for a while. Then he told me he had a script and suggested that I audition. I told him I wasn't a professional actress.

"It couldn't hurt to try," he said.

Kenny explained that the understudies only did matinees to smaller audiences. The leading characters did the evening performances to the larger crowds. I felt better when I heard that and agreed to read the script and come back in a couple of weeks.

By the time I finished talking to Kenny, the cast had gone backstage, but I saw David walking out the front door. He was just as Barbara had described him—handsome, with

163

curly black hair and a chocolate face with deep dimples embedded in both sides of his cheeks and a Kirk Douglas cleft in the middle of his chin. We stared at each other, but didn't speak.

To my surprise, I got a warm response to my audition, and when they offered me the part, I cried. At first I truly didn't believe that I could do it. Having been raised in a predominately white environment, I feared other blacks wouldn't accept me. But when I went to rehearsal, the entire cast made me feel welcome, and I basked in the sense of belonging. I got to know everyone in the cast except David, who wasn't around because I would be acting opposite his understudy, Fred. My first matinee performances were frightening, but eventually I settled into the part and did quite well. I discovered that singing and acting went hand in hand.

Everything changed a few weeks later when Barbara got in a car accident. She wasn't critically hurt, but she was bruised and wouldn't be able to do the show on the upcoming Friday. As her understudy, I had to take over, but I wasn't ready for that responsibility, and I was afraid to act opposite David. The few times I had seen him in passing, he had seemed distant and preoccupied. We had never spoken to each other.

Since I had performed a few times already, there was no need to rehearse with David. All I had to do was act the same way I did with Fred, but I was nervous all week waiting for Friday to roll around. When it did, the theater was packed. I went to the dressing room and tried to calm down, and the cast rallied around and encouraged me when they saw how frightened I was.

I was sitting and quietly praying, so I didn't see David come into the room. Then I heard a deep, reassuring voice say, "Relax, you're going to do fine."

When the lights came on, somehow I did my part. The cast was proud of me afterward, and David congratulated me. "Good job," he said.

The more I worked with David, the more I liked him. If he had any feelings toward me, he never let on. He was fun loving and outgoing with the other cast members, but he was distant toward me, and I figured he didn't like me. One of the girls in the cast told me that he had a girlfriend but that they weren't doing well and had broken up. Well, he wasn't married, but the interest that other fair maidens had in him brought back memories of JB. I didn't want to get hurt, so I put David out of my mind.

A month later our relationship changed. We were having new pictures taken of the cast. David was warmer toward me during that session, and we started talking more after the shows. Eventually we started to try to spend more time together, although it was hard with so many people vying for his attention. I should have taken my clue from seeing the many directions he was pulled in, but I didn't.

One evening my friend Prescott, from the band The Knack, was playing bass at a club in Santa Monica. He asked me to come see him play, and I asked David to go. To my surprise he said yes. From that evening on, we were inseparable. Once it was under way, our relationship accelerated at the speed of a runaway freight train.

David was twenty-five when we started dating; I was twenty-seven. Joseph had never showed any real interest in my male friends. He was courteous but never tried to get close to them. That changed when he met David. Joseph warmed up to him immediately.

My mother, however, wasn't pleased that we were seeing so much of each other. She thought our relationship was moving too fast, and we argued about it. It was hard for her to understand my impulsiveness, and she warned me to take things slowly. When she angrily pointed out all my faults, it drove a wedge between us and pushed me farther away. In hindsight, it must have been devastating for her to watch me go from one chaotic situation to another. I know she was trying to spare me the pain she had suffered in her life, but she didn't know how to talk to me.

I continued to see David despite obvious red flags. He witnessed the vicious fighting going on between my mother and me, and I noticed that he drank too much beer. We were both carrying unresolved baggage. I needed to deal with my volatile past; he needed to come to terms with his drinking. We cared for each other, but I don't think either one of us ever thought our relationship would go as far as it did.

One night while we were on a date, David told me he had to tell me something. My heart sank because I thought he was going to tell me that he was married. I closed my eyes and braced myself for the worst. He told me that he and his girlfriend of four years had planned to go their separate ways. She had moved out but had then discovered that she was pregnant. The baby was due in a month.

We talked for hours about his situation. I knew deep inside that our relationship was not right under these circumstances; still I couldn't imagine life without him. The tables had turned on me. I was now where Cathy had been five years earlier, but my choices weren't as noble as hers.

One of six children, David had been raised in a Christian home. His father was a minister, and the family attended church regularly, but David wasn't going to church when I met him. I had not backslid in four years, but after I met David I went right back to my old pattern. My life had to be confusing to him. On the one hand I was encouraging him to go back to church, while on the other I was involved in a sexual relationship with him. I knew better than to believe that if we went to church together, God would overlook our disobedience to His Word.

When I told my mother about David's girlfriend, Shelly, she said, "If you love each other, you need to wait." She told me that I needed to give David some time before our relationship went any further. She felt that he was probably afraid to be a new father and warned me that he would not know how he truly felt until his baby was born. He might in fact realize that he still loved the mother of his child. If not, he would at least have time to sort things out.

I knew that my mother's counsel was sound and from the Lord. David and I agreed not to see each other until his baby was born and he had worked things out with his girlfriend. I was getting ready to go to Las Vegas to sing background for José Feliciano. I would be gone for a few weeks, and my intentions were to fast and pray and wait for God's guidance. I couldn't stop crying. David had made a terrible choice getting involved with me under the circumstances, and I knew he wouldn't abandon his responsibility like JB had. I believed with all my heart that once he saw his new baby, I would probably never see him again.

David had agreed to stay behind, but during the last week of my engagement in Vegas, he came there with his younger brother and a friend. He told me that he was afraid I wouldn't wait for him. He was determined to be in his baby's life, but he didn't want to lose me. Two nights later after my show we impulsively and irresponsibly went to a justice of the peace and got married.

David and I had been dating only a month. When we filled out the forms for our marriage license, neither one of us even knew the full names of our prospective in-laws. We didn't know anything personal about each other. He had no idea where I was born; I knew nothing about his past or family. Two strangers stood before a solemn old man inside a cold courthouse and made vows we were in no way prepared to keep.

After we got married and went back to my room, we stared at each other like two kids who had just robbed a bank. Our eyes widened in disbelief at what we had just done. When David went to sleep, I lay beside him thinking about a dream I had had when I first started dating him. In it, we were holding hands as we walked toward the sunlight. All of a sudden a huge black cloud passed over us, and thunderous rain and wind blew us apart. After the storm moved out of the area, we slowly found each other and held hands again. I saw a big storm ahead of us, and my prayer was that we would make it in the end. I knew we were going to face consequences for hurting David's girlfriend, not to mention our two unsuspecting mothers back in LA.

It didn't take long for the storm clouds to appear on the horizon. At 6:00 AM the telephone rang. It was my mother. "The Lord woke me up around three o clock this morning," she said. "I had a heavy burden on my heart for you. I don't know what you've done, Lolita, but your decision is going to cost you."

I wanted to tell her what I had done, but I couldn't. I was in shock. No one knew that David was there with me, so the Lord had obviously spoken to her heart when I got married. I lied and told her that everything was fine.

169

Chapter Fifteen

REPENT AT LEISURE

When David left Las Vegas, I was sure he would regret getting married, and I prepared myself to never hear from him again. When I got home, however, he sent me a dozen yellow roses welcoming me. He and I both thought it best not to say anything until we figured out how to break the news. His first child was due any day, and he decided he would tell Shelly after she had the baby.

At that point things got even more complicated. I felt tired and sick after my trip, but I didn't think anything of it until I missed my period. I had been regular for years, so I knew I was pregnant. Having another baby was only going to add more fuel to the fire. My only consolation was that I was married.

At first, I kept all of my emotions pent up and tried to carry on with life as usual. I would go to the park after I dropped Joe off at school and sit in my car, cry, and pray until it was time to pick him up. I didn't want to be around my family because I didn't want anyone to suspect anything. With each passing day, however, I was increasingly tormented by the seriousness of my situation. After a while, I couldn't stand the stress any longer, and I told my younger brother and a cousin that I was married and expecting a baby. My brother gave me a hug and congratulated me. "I hope you know what you're doing." he said. My cousin's jaw dropped. What could she say?

I eventually told David I was pregnant because I had become insanely jealous that he was taking Shelly to Lamaze classes. He got very quiet. He tried to reassure me that everything would work out and told me to be patient. So I kept a low profile and continued to live with my mother.

Late one evening, David called me to tell me that his daughter had just been born. Excited, he told me how beautiful she was. I was happy for him, but I could tell from his voice that something unexpected had happened. David had watched the birth of his daughter and had already bonded with her. The depth of emotion and love he already felt for her seems to have surprised even him. My mother's words came back to haunt me. She had warned me that David might have conflicting feelings once his first child was born.

I, on the other hand, had childishly believed that once the baby was born, David would switch gears and concentrate on building our new life together. It had been too long since I'd seen him, and I wanted him to come and spend some time with me, but he told me that he couldn't just run off and leave his daughter. He would come over as soon as he could get away.

David was irritated at being pulled in two different directions. Staring his dilemma straight in the face, he dealt with the facts. Shelly and his daughter's needs had to come first; mine had to take a backseat. Not only had I cheated myself out of a wedding and honeymoon, but I had also ended up with a conflicted groom. Had the Lord's will been done, my marriage could have been a joyous occasion for all. Now it felt more like a funeral. I guess in many ways it was.

I had gotten myself into this mess, and now I had to figure a way out of it. I figured I was going to end up raising my two children alone, and I knew I couldn't keep living with my mother. I started looking in the paper to find a place to move to. When I couldn't stand the pain and guilt any longer, I told my mother that I was married and expecting another baby. She was speechless. I don't think she could believe that I could possibly have been so heartless.

173

"You of all people should know how that girl feels," she said, speaking of my disregard for Shelly's feelings. She told me something my grandmother used to say: "You can't tap dance on someone else's grave."

I had no argument. She was one 100 percent right. Five years ago I had been in Shelly's shoes. How could I have done this? I never meant to hurt her. She and David weren't married, and he had told me they had broken up. All those thoughts raced through my mind. I wasn't totally to blame for all that had transpired, but whether David was married or not, I should have given him time to see where his heart truly lay. It wasn't that I didn't care about Shelly's feelings; it was just that, as with any true addict, my fix came first. I couldn't imagine life without David.

I could tell by my mother's expression that she was crushed. She told me to go call my husband. Feeling numb and detached, I called David. My mother asked to speak to him.

"Come and get your wife and family," she said calmly.

As I went upstairs to pack, a sharp pain stabbed my heart. I wept as I packed Joseph's and my things. I kept thinking, *What have I done? My life wasn't supposed to turn out like this. Why am I so screwed up? How could I hurt so many people?* I knew my mother had to be disgusted with me. God had gotten me out of the situation I had gotten into with JB, and here I was in another one. I really felt bad when I realized that I was uprooting Joseph from the only security he had ever known. At the time I didn't realize that I was repeating the dysfunctional patterns from my past, doing the same painful things to my son that had been done to me.

As we gathered Joe's toys, I told him that I was married and that he now had a new daddy. I had at least prepared him over the years for the fact that one day a man would enter our lives. I hadn't wanted him totally taken off guard as I had been. When he found out that David was now his father, he smilingly packed his little toys. If he was frightened or concerned about leaving his grandmother and uncles and friends in the neighborhood, he never showed it. He went along like a little trooper. Only years later would I learn that Joe suffered from the abrupt changes forced upon him, but I am comforted by the fact that I kept him close to me as much as possible and that he liked David a lot.

I felt despondent as we waited for David to pick us up. I imagine he thought he was coming for his twenty-seven-year-old wife and his new five-year-old son, but in reality, he was picking up two children. I sat on my bed looking out the bedroom window. When I saw David's little red car pull up and park in front of the house, my heart practically leaped out of my chest. I felt so relieved to see him; he was going to fix everything.

My mother was quiet, but I saw the hurt and anger in her face. I knew she was devastated that Joseph was being taken away. There were tears in her eyes as David took our things to the car. She could scarcely look at me. I think she felt that I was purposely trying to hurt and defy her, but I wasn't. I was desperately seeking love and a sense of belonging, and I thought that having my own family would fill that aching need. I believe that many young women think marriage can transform half a person into a whole one. Trust me, it can't.

Feeling like a zombie, I took Joseph from the only security he had ever known, left my family, friends, and brothers and sisters in the Lord, and gave up what little claim I had to being in my own world with my own identity. David would have to be strong for all of us. We didn't have mutual friends or community. We had traveled down different paths, and I was replacing Shelly, someone his peers knew well. What better way to heap more hate upon myself than to walk into my new husband's world as the other woman!

David and I were distant in the car. I think both of us were full of remorse. Before he drove me to his apartment, we toured the neighborhood where his parents and two of his sisters lived.

He showed me around so I could get familiar with the surroundings. He pointed to different houses and told me who lived where and what his relationship was with them. I felt as if we were two criminals casing the joint, trying to find a way to sneak into his family incognito.

David finally decided to stop and tell his parents. I sat looking at their spacious three-story house against the dark backdrop of the evening, praying they would accept me. The neighborhood, it in a soft yellow hue, was the picture of serenity and peace. I wasn't. My heart was pounding in my chest, and I wanted to cry, but it was time to face the music.

David's dad hugged him when he saw him. His older sister was there with her three children. They were talking to David, not expecting company. Then David stepped out of the way, and there stood Joseph and I. His mother was taken off guard, but she smiled. David asked his parents if we could speak to them in private. His sister had a puzzled expression on her face. She walked downstairs to the family room, taking Joseph with her. David and I went upstairs to his parents' room.

By now they both had concerned expressions on their faces, and the atmosphere was solemn and still. "What's wrong?" his mother asked.

As David introduced me as his new wife, I looked down at my hands, totally embarrassed. His parents stared at us. It was quiet in the room for a while, and then the questions began. They wanted to know how long we had known each other. With each perfectly logical question they asked, the more irresponsible I felt. David's mother's main concern was for Shelly and the baby. She told David that he needed to tell her promptly. His parents were patient with us but expressed their disappointment with our lack of discretion.

Then his father asked us to pray. We bowed our heads as he asked God for His wisdom and guidance in the situation. His prayer was convicting and brought tears to my eyes. My new father-in-law was right—only the Lord Himself could rectify the circumstances. There was nothing anyone could do or say to change what had already taken place. When we went downstairs and David introduced me to his older sister, she reacted with total shock.

After we left his parents house, we headed for the apartment David had once shared with Shelly. They had found it together. I felt anxious and disoriented when we arrived. I didn't know what to do with myself. I looked around the place, knowing full well that I didn't belong there. David and I talked for a long time. He was stressed but trying hard to reassure me that he could be a vital part of his daughter's life and still be a husband and father to our children. I wanted to believe him, but it was a pretty tall order for any young couple.

The news began to spread that David was married. I was thrust upon David's siblings and friends, and no one knew how to respond to me. On the whole, I'd have to say that people were cordial to me. There were those who rolled their eyes when I walked into a room and whispered behind my back, but what did I expect? It must have been difficult getting to know me without feeling they were betraying Shelly. Shelly and her family were furious and let it be known. I think they believed that David's family knew about our marriage all along, even though they didn't. Because of our narcissistic actions, there was discord, tension, and anger between the two families.

I watched the events unfolding around me through a fog of detachment. As time went on, the dust settled and I was accepted, but there was a great strain on our marriage. I might have fared better had I been more secure. But I had so many injuries of my own that I didn't handle the challenges in a diplomatic fashion.

I was coming in cold from the outside into a family system that already had a set way of interacting. David's family was a close, tight-knit group similar to my family in Chicago. They were like a little city in and of themselves. They had one another's company and didn't need to interact with outsiders. They were also fun loving, with a keen sense of humor, and knew how to have a good time. Their community of friends and church members spent a great deal of time visiting. Ironically, just as my family's good times centered on alcohol, so did David's.

Since David's family hadn't moved as often as mine, he had more attachments to his surroundings and a sense of belonging. Our major marital problems would be due to that one dynamic alone. David had affirmation coming from all directions. The people at the theater adored him. His entire family held him in high esteem. He was handsome, hilarious, bright, creative, and articulate and helped see his family through difficult times. Friends and neighbors alike wanted to be around the family. In fact, David's parents' home was the place to be.

I believe that David often sought autonomy and separateness, but people were always around, trying to be close and hang out with him. On the other hand, I had not had the opportunity to form long-lasting bonds and attachments in any community and had always felt lonely. David feared suffocation; I feared abandonment. Our union was a keg of dynamite waiting to explode.

I thought that marriage would fill that empty longing in my heart, and I felt threatened by all of the people around David. I wanted to be the priority in my husband's life, and I started pulling at him for attention and trying to build a fence around both of us. As I competed with the others for a place in his heart, I became demanding, controlling, and jealous of the time he spent away from me. My insistence on his loyalty and dedication only pushed him farther away. The more I cried and argued with him about spending special time together, the more he withdrew. He began to feel trapped by my demands, and his silence infuriated me.

179

The attention and affirmation I sought was biblical, but the way I tried to get it wasn't. The Bible says that a man "will leave his father and mother and be united to his wife, and they will become one flesh" (Genesis 2:24). I didn't have a biblical marriage. Maybe if David and I had waited upon the Lord and allowed Him to move in our hearts and gradually bring us together as a couple, we would have had a stable marriage. God could have shown us how to handle our new circumstances. However, you can't break God's ordinances, hurt others in the process, and then expect the Lord to bless you. But I was still a citizen of Neptune, and as usual, I thought that since I wanted everything to just magically fall into place, it would. Of course, it didn't.

For personal reasons, David ended up buying his parents' home, and we moved into the big house with them. His mother and I worked as a team doing the housework and shopping, and we prayed together whenever possible. Both my in-laws took Joseph back and forth to school and were the loving second set of grandparents he desperately needed. David proved to be a good father to Joseph. Under the circumstances, the arrangement worked out well, but it didn't give David and me the opportunity to forge a new life together, and the road was rocky as I waited to have our baby. We loved each other in our own way, but neither one of us had the emotional resources we needed to keep from stumbling.

By my sixth month of pregnancy, I was settling more into the structure and routine of our new life, and David and I began taking late-night drives and spending special time together. It meant a lot to me whenever David made arrangements for Joseph to stay with my mother so we could take weekend trips to San Francisco, San Diego, or Santa Barbara. It helped ease the stress and tension, and I began to feel more secure.

During one of my prenatal visits, I discovered that I had a condition called *placenta previa*. My placenta had detached from the wall of my uterus and was covering the birth canal. Had I gone into labor, the placenta would have delivered first and suffocated the baby, and I could have bled to death. When the time came to give birth, I would have to have a cesarean section. In the meantime I had to take it easy and stay off my feet to make sure I didn't go into premature labor.

A few weeks before my baby was born, David surprised

me by coming home early from work. I knew something was wrong by the solemn expression on his face. My mother had called him earlier and told him that my cousin Moe had been killed in a motorcycle accident. David wanted to be the one to tell me. Moe and I had been close since he lived with my family during high school.

I was stunned. I could scarcely believe that he was dead. Six months before his death, I had dreamed that violence was all around him but that the Lord was going to take care of him. I earnestly sought the Lord in prayer on Moe's behalf after that dream. A few months later, someone stabbed him in a park, but he survived. I was so relieved he lived. I thought that the trouble was over.

My mother and I had both witnessed to Moe while he was recuperating in the hospital. He eventually gave his heart to the Lord. The only comfort I had after his death was knowing that he was with the Lord and that God had assured me He would take care of him. I cried for weeks after the tragedy. I couldn't attend the funeral because of the complications of my pregnancy.

On some of my prenatal visits, I saw my doctor's partner. An elderly physician, he told me that he had been listening to fetal heartbeats for more than forty years and that he guessed by the rate of my baby's heartbeat that I was carrying a little girl. I had forgotten all about the Scripture I had read years earlier that had convinced me I would have sons.

I already loved my baby, no matter what the sex. However, I would be happy to have a daughter. I told David what the doctor said. We agreed on the name Blair Elise. I loved the name Blair, from the character Lisa Whelchel played on the hit television show at the time, *The Facts of Life*. Then one night I had a dream that David's younger brother came up to me holding a blue suit for a little boy.

"The baby is a boy," he said.

I argued with him in the dream that the doctor said the baby was a girl. The dream clearly depicted my relationship with the Lord. I was always in conflict in terms of trusting Him. I relied on what the doctor said and believed I was going to have a girl. However, I wasn't convinced enough to tell everyone to get all girl things!

Over the next couple of months, the Lord gave me the opportunity to begin to make amends to Shelly. When she brought her beautiful baby girl Charmaine over to see her father, I asked Shelly to step outside so that we could talk. I wanted her to know that I was not the reason for their breakup. David met me after the fact. Still, I shouldn't have married him under the circumstances.

We had a long private conversation. I told her how sorry I was for hurting her. I was impressed by her strength. However she dealt with her feelings in private, she handled the situation with dignity in public. She was forthright in telling David what she expected from him with regard to taking care of their child, and he fulfilled his responsibility out of deep love for his daughter.

A year later, I swallowed my pride and apologized to my mother for having hurt her so deeply, and I told her that her counsel had turned out to be painfully true. I was glad that I apologized for my wrongdoings. I felt tremendous peace because I never wanted anyone to be upset or angry with me, but I was also sad that no one ever came to me to ask for my forgiveness for having hurt me. I had to eventually let go of that wish.

It wasn't that difficult to admit I was wrong. I had always felt that I was a terrible person and that anything bad that ever happened was my fault. I already knew I was a failure. Unfortunately no one but the Lord understood why I was so self-destructive, and He was patiently waiting for me to hit bottom. He didn't have long to wait.

Chapter Sixteen

ROCK BOTTOM

On December 9, 1983, my second son was born. So much for the doctor's forty years of experience predicting the sex of a baby by listening to heart rates. And so much for trusting the doctor instead of God! David and I changed the name Blair Elise to Nicholas Edward. I loved that name from the little boy on the hit television show *Eight Is Enough.* (Who says television doesn't influence people?) The name means "victor of the people." David wanted a unique spelling, so he spelled it Nikolas.

During the birth, David and I were closer than ever. He was with me during the entire operation and saw the doctor pushing my body parts aside to get to the baby. Later on he joked that he now knew me inside and out. I drew comfort and strength from having him there as I went through the frightening ordeal of having a cesarean. He reassured me when things got stressful, and his comedic ways lightened the atmosphere. And I didn't feel alone and ashamed, as I had as an unwed mother. I now had my own family, and I felt proud when my husband came to the hospital. It touched me deeply to see how excited he was to have a son and how loving and supportive of me he was.

As we adjusted to being a blended family, things were peaceful between David and me for a while. We began taking family trips with our three children. I felt secure and special in his life when it was just our family, but when it came time to go back home and face the other responsibilities and commitments we had, things got tense and we argued.

I didn't know how to discuss problems diplomatically. I either kept things bottled up inside and tried to smile, or I went ballistic and stomped around like a madwoman. Never mind that I had the worst timing in the world to bring up my concerns. I'd pick happy occasions, as when we were out for a romantic drive or movie, to discuss painful issues. David didn't like to argue, so he withdrew and used silence to shut me out, which infuriated me even more. Our relationship began to unravel, and I slowly became aware that I had serious emotional problems.

It troubled me how dependent I was on David. I was like a child. It was as though I had never survived on my own before I met him. I had at least been financially independent before we got married, and I had never allowed myself to need anyone that much. Nor had I ever given anyone, not even JB, my full heart. But I gave David that and much more. As a result, I needed constant reassurance that he loved me and would never leave me. I had left all of my friends behind and made him my connection to the world, and I clung to him like a drowning person holding on to the lifeguard.

My in-laws were loved and respected by the entire community, and our home was open to all. That left almost no time for David and me to be close as a couple. Weekends were fun and exciting because it was like a party with all the people David's family knew. But at times I felt jealous because the friends of the family were a constant reminder that I was an outsider.

I was irritable and impatient with my kids, especially Joseph. I was strict with him and disciplined him harshly. I never wanted to give the outside world the appearance that anything was wrong between David and me. I felt others were expecting our house of cards to fall soon, and I looked to Joseph to shine brightly as proof that we were doing just fine as a family.

I did all I could to maintain the facade of being a happy, Jesus-praising, people-pleasing person. I tried hard to mask my needs and cries for help by comforting other people and minding their business. My mood swings from smiling and preaching Christ to venting my rage frightened even me. I felt like I was having a nervous breakdown—and I probably was.

187

The only thing I knew to do was to pray earnestly to the Lord. After I took Joseph to school, I would put Nikolas in his stroller and walk around the neighborhood for hours praying. People must have thought I was loony talking to myself like that, but I didn't care. I was crying out to the Lord for help.

As time went on, David and I moved miles apart emotionally. He was struggling with alcohol and feeling trapped. I wanted a Christian home and family, but I had laid no foundation for the Lord to build upon. I told God that I didn't want a divorce.

I had gotten myself in trouble; I wasn't going to make matters worse by adding divorce to my other sins.

My children were reaping the consequences of my instability. Joseph was angry and having behavioral problems in school. He was lashing out at the other students and having major conflict with his female teachers. Nikolas was a fussy baby. As I lamented over the condition of my children, I was also falling apart.

I began having panic attacks. One time when I was sitting in my car looking for gas money, all of a sudden I grabbed onto the steering wheel and started perspiring heavily. I thought the car had started moving on its own. It hadn't, for the motor wasn't even running. I also began having chest pains, and on more than one occasion I had to go to the hospital. Each time I was told that my symptoms were stress related. I lost hair and had terrible skin and other stress-related symptoms that wouldn't clear up.

In the midst of all this turmoil, I continued crying out to the Lord for help. I tried attending churches, but I changed them like socks. When people got to know my children too well, I'd leave the church. I wasn't interested in getting close to anyone. I preferred to be left alone. It was painful conversing with others after service. I always came late, sat in the back of the church, and was the first one to leave. I went to five different churches in one year alone.

I started to take a lot of Nyquil to help me sleep, but then I'd wake up and find that David wasn't home. Even if it was a school night, I'd get the boys out of bed, put them in the car, and drive around in a sleepy fog looking for David. It was only by the grace of God that I didn't kill myself or someone else. Usually, I'd end up at my mother's.

My mother was accommodating and always glad to see her grandsons, but there was still unresolved bitterness and anger between us. When I could no longer stand the pressure of staying with her, I'd drag the boys back home to their father. I was lost, and my innocent children paid the price. It must have been terrifying for them to have to rely on some- one emotionally younger than they were to take care of them.

Over a period of time, my mother saw how distraught I was over the condition of my marriage, and she gave me a book that gave me hope: *Love Must Be Tough*, by Dr. James Dobson. As I pored over the pages, I saw myself and recognized all the controlling, manipulating patterns that were driving David and me further and further apart. God gave me insight into David's behavior, as well. I read that book over and over again and tried to follow Dr. Dobson's advice. I prayed, asking God to show me what to do.

David and I were separated for the summer, and one night while I was sleeping at my mother's house, I woke up at four in the morning. I remember because I looked at the clock radio on the nightstand.

A gentle voice called out my name. "Lolita."

I sat up in bed and looked around the dark room. I wasn't afraid, just perplexed. I cleared my eyes so I could see into the room, but no one was there. I figured I had been dreaming, so I started to doze off again, when I heard the same voice say, "The problem is alcoholism."

I sat up and turned on the light. I thought about what I had just heard. *What is alcoholism?* I asked myself. I wasn't a drinker and had no idea what it was all about. People in my family drank, but I didn't think any were alcoholics. Despite his drinking binges, my grandfather never missed a day of work. I don't remember my grandmother ever drinking. My mother was not drinking to excess as she once had, and the violence had stopped. David was never abusive when he drank beer. In fact, he was friendlier and more outgoing. When he was sober, he was subdued and distant, as my grandfather had been.

Like most people, I equated alcoholics with homeless, skid row bums. I had yet to learn that only about 3 percent of alcoholics fall into that category. Many are pillars of their communities—intelligent, charismatic, creative people with great jobs and loving families.

I didn't tell anyone what had happened. Having dreams was one thing; hearing voices was another. I thought I'd be locked up for sure if I told folks that one. I had a raging conflict going on inside. Was that God who had spoken to me, or not?

The next day I decided to buy a book on alcoholism. I put two-year-old Nik in his stroller and walked up the street to the little village bookstore. I purposely looked in the Christian section because I didn't want to be led astray in my search for answers, and I browsed around, looking for the right book. Suddenly one caught my attention: *Getting Them Sober*, by Toby Rice Drews.

When I read the foreword and the first few chapters (they were very short chapters), I just about dropped to my knees right there in the store. It was as if the author had taken a camera and followed me throughout my life. I bought both volumes, and I could hardly wait to get back to my mother's to read them. That afternoon, it was as if the Lord handed me a playbook of every destructive, mean, and hateful tactic the enemy had been using against my family for years. Each page described the attitudes and behaviors of people I had grown up with.

I was dismayed by the devastating consequences to the loved ones of people who use alcohol (or drugs, food, sex, or spending) to medicate themselves amidst the pain of life. It stabbed my heart when I discovered that alcoholism is a family affair and that anyone who is closely associated with any kind of addicted person can have profound emotional injuries.

I saw my own hostile, out-of-control behavior and how my actions were perpetuating the craziness that had gone on in my home. I began to recognize how badly the kids and I needed help. I kept my Bible, *Love Must Be Tough*, and *Getting Them Sober* by my bed. I reached for one of them the minute my eyes opened in the morning, and I took them everywhere I went. Many nights when I woke up crying, I reached for one of them for comfort.

For the first time in my life, I felt that someone knew what was wrong with me and where I could get help. The Lord had known all along that alcoholism was one of the things behind my many problems, but He had patiently waited until I reached rock bottom and would finally listen to Him. Now He had my full attention.

Of course, I tried to cram my new insights down everyone's throat. I thought people would be happy and excited when I told them, "Hey, guys, our family is sick and needs help." However, I soon discovered that they took offense at the insinuation that they might be alcoholics or have emotional problems. I found out that in some cases it was much easier for people to extend me grace when I was lost and out of control than it was to support me as I began to walk down a different path.

Once I had gotten mad at David and smeared birthday cake all over his car and windshield, embarrassing my kids and myself. Another time, bright and early in the morning, I had stood outside in my nightgown yelling at him. I thought people would be thrilled that I was finally taking steps to do something about the problems that caused such behavior, but to my surprise, I met great resistance. The cold shoulder I got from some people took me aback, but I continued to rejoice over the path I was about to embark on. I had found out that there were people who understood my destructive behavior, and I wanted to find them and ask them to please help me.

I made up my mind that I didn't want to pass any more destruction on to my children. I told the Lord that even if no one else wanted to hear it, my boys and I were getting help. I had been alone emotionally all my life. What would be different about getting help alone? I had walked down dark, depressing roads; it had to be a better deal to walk down a lighted path, even if I had to walk it alone.

In her book, Drews suggested that families could find answers and relief from the pain of having lived with problem drinkers at Al-Anon meetings, so I went back and read what Dr. Dobson had to say about Al-Anon. In a chapter dealing with families affected by alcoholism, he included the story of a couple named Bob and Pauline. Pauline told how she had stopped arguing with Bob about his drinking. Instead, she had left him alone and gotten help for herself. Eventually Bob got help, too, and together they started a Christian 12-step ministry called Overcomers Anonymous.

Dr. Dobson said that both Al-Anon and Overcomers could help people from families where alcoholism was a problem. A few days later, God confirmed the path I should take. I was driving along listening to the radio when a commercial for Al-Anon came on. "Okay, okay," I told the Lord, "three times is enough. I'm going." A few days later, I picked up the phone and called the main office for Al-Anon. A really nice man shared his story with me and told me where the meeting nearest to my mother's was.

My first meeting was at a church near UCLA. I was terrified to go alone, but I had made up my mind that I could no longer live the way I had been. The room was packed with people drinking coffee and laughing and talking. At first I thought I was in the wrong room. I wondered how they could be so happy if they were suffering from the effects of alcoholism. I found a seat and sat quietly until the meeting began. When a young girl got up and introduced herself as the leader of that night's meeting, I almost swallowed my teeth. I recognized her immediately. I didn't know her personally, but at the time she was a major character on a hit television series.

You've got to be kidding, I thought. *What's she doing here? She's famous, with a lot of money and success. She couldn't possibly be suffering.*

"Hi, my name is Carla," she said, "and I'm an adult child of an alcoholic." When the perky blonde identified herself as an adult child of an alcoholic parent, I soaked up the information like a sponge. As she told her story, I no longer saw a celebrity. I saw a wounded woman whose childhood had been a lot like mine. Her mother had stopped drinking, but their relationship was tumultuous from years of chaos and abuse. She rattled off a long list of the crazy, destructive patterns and toxic love relationships that had painfully impacted her life. Then she spoke of finding Al-Anon and the tremendous difference it had made ever since.

I wanted to leap out of my chair and kiss her after she spoke. Her vulnerability and transparency stunned me. Secrecy and hiding were all I knew. Never in my life had I heard anyone, much less a celebrity, reveal so much personal information.

When other members began sharing their stories, I recognized my dysfunctional love patterns in just about every one of them. Some people had known their husband or wife one day before they got married. I thought that David and I had done the unspeakable by getting married after knowing each other for six weeks. Other young women cried about getting involved over and over again with men like JB in their destructive search for love. Some people told how family members had sexually abused them.

As the meeting continued, I remember thinking, *My God, all this time I thought I was the only one who felt like this.* Now I realized that much of my behavior was a classic symptom of the problems that plagued my childhood and family. I lowered my head and whispered a silent prayer of relief and gratitude that God had led me to Al-Anon.

Chapter Seventeen

A DIFFERENT PATH

I continued to attend weekly Al-Anon meetings while David and I were separated for the summer. Each time I attended a meeting and read the literature, I discovered many things about myself. Proverbs 14:1 says, "The wise woman builds her house, but with her own hands the foolish one tears hers down." In many ways, I was like that foolish woman. I wasn't the sole contributor to our martial discord, but I was certainly responsible for part of it, and I knew that one day I would have to account to God for my own behavior, not someone else's. It became very clear that I had to make major attitude adjustments.

The Lord sent people to help me. On many occasions, help came in meetings from the wise elderly souls we called "the old-timers," individuals who had been in recovery for more than twenty years. Whenever they imparted the wisdom they had gained from years of experience, it was like getting a cold drink of water on a hot, parched day.

One woman in particular helped me. One night after a meeting, I told her about my struggles and the resistance I was receiving from loved ones. "Your family members are adults," she said, "and you must treat them as such. Don't try to force them to see things your way. Let God change you first." Her advice helped me to see that I was concentrating on managing others when I should have been focusing on what a mess my own life was. I now wanted to take stock of myself.

When I began attending Al-Anon in the fall of 1985, I wasn't familiar with the term *codependency,* but I soon discovered how much I was plagued by it. For years I had put others' feelings and wishes before mine in destructive ways. Afraid to truly stand up for what I believed, I made situations possible that I knew weren't right.

I always tried to hide what was going on inside. Sometimes I was successful; other times not. I'd stuff emotions down for a long time and then explode at the least provocation. Most of the time, I felt more at home living in the eye of a hurricane than I did in a peaceful atmosphere. Ironically, I never wanted to make anyone angry, but I did so many impulsive things that I ended up hurting others and bringing controversy to my own front door regularly.

I felt guilty and responsible for how others felt and often searched frantically to find ways to fix their lives. I displaced my own emotions and channeled my energies into other people's affairs. Even as I encouraged people to depend on me, I was resentful when they did and felt they were taking advantage of me.

I thought that a good Christian strove for peace at any

price and helped anyone in trouble. I believed that bearing one another's burdens meant supporting struggling souls and helping them overcome obstacles. But I found out that there is a huge difference between being a servant of Christ by laying one's life down and taking responsibility for capable adults. Jesus commanded us to pick up our own cross and follow Him. He never told us to carry other people's crosses.

In layman terms, I learned that I had to get out of the Lord's way. I wasn't God, and I certainly wasn't responsible for how the world wagged. I could care deeply, but not to the point of managing others' lives and neglecting my own. I had to learn how to mind my own business and not worry about how others perceived me.

197

David and I were corresponding during our separation, and we made plans to take a trip with another couple at the end of the summer. The four of us were going to travel up the coast to Santa Barbara for a week. For David and me, it was to be both a time of reconciliation and the honeymoon we had never had. Before then, I had a lot of emotional work to do, for I was determined to go back home equipped with the new principles I was learning.

The time came when David and I reconciled and went on our trip, leaving the boys with my mother. It was a refreshing reprieve from the stress of the previous months. I was so happy to be back with my husband enjoying our special time together, and I was truly optimistic about our future. I prayed earnestly that when we returned home, David would enter the healing process with me. I so wanted the Lord to restore our family.

While we were on vacation, we talked about the mistakes we had both made. I promised to stop nagging him about not spending enough time with the boys and me and to work on my insecurities, especially when he dealt with Shelly. I was still having a hard time because David wouldn't take me along when we attended his daughter's school activities or events where he had to interact with Shelly's family. Our marriage had been a painful blow to Shelly and her family, and David wanted peace with them for the sake of his daughter, but I couldn't help feeling excluded.

There were other areas of concern. I wanted to set up our own household. I loved David's family and not getting along was never the issue. The problem was that thus far David and I hadn't bonded as a couple, and we needed privacy to work out our problems. We were both still emotionally attached to our families of origin. I knew I had to start unraveling my own ties, and I wanted David to take steps toward more independence by moving into our own home. David saw our struggles differently. He didn't want to move or go to Al-Anon meetings. I think we were both under the illusion that through sheer willpower we could overcome all our obstacles by changing the other. We didn't realize that our patterns of discourse were set as hard as cement.

When we returned home, I decided to forge a life for myself and keep working on me. Learning not to look to David as my sole source of company and emotional support was painful, but I knew I had to take a more active role in finding the answers for my own life.

Unfortunately, I continued to church hop. I still didn't feel safe sharing my intimate struggles with a church family. I found that some believers weren't comfortable dealing with gutbucket honesty or relating to emotions other than joy. Negative, painful sharing was to them just speaking defeat. I felt that such people were looking for sisters and brothers who had mastered the Christian walk and already shone like gems. That certainly wasn't me, so I'd attend the "church of the month" until people started to know me, and then off I'd run.

I carried that behavior into other aspects of my life as well. If people got to know my face too well at a bank, cleaners, or grocery store, I'd stop going. (I still battle those feelings today.) I didn't know why I did it; I just knew that I always felt safer being unknown. I wanted the freedom to be seen, but yet not.

199

I found an Al-Anon group that met at a hospital near my home, and it became my home meeting. The Lord brought some special women into my life, and I grew to love and cherish them. I took baby steps towards letting my Sunday night sisters get a glimpse inside me because they were fellow sufferers who understood what I was going through. It was easier to peek out of my hole because I knew they were taking risks, too.

I eventually found my first sponsor there. Gert was a petite, gentle black woman with inner strength and character. I didn't choose her because of color; she just happened to be a woman of color. With the exception of a few incidents while I was growing up, race had never been an issue with me in life (still isn't). I chose Gert because I admired her. I loved her spirit, and I wanted to learn from her how to be more self-assured, yet not so abrasive when I got angry.

I visited Gert's home regularly as I worked through the

twelve steps with her. She and her husband had their own struggles, but they each worked separate 12-step programs, attended church together, and went through counseling. There was a respect and teamwork in their relationship that I hadn't often witnessed in marriages. I wanted to learn how to relate in healthier ways in my own marriage. In many ways, I still behaved like a child. At times I flew off the handle, trying to get in the last word. I wanted to mature.

I was slowly finding a direction for myself and building a network of support. When David visited the neighbors or his family, I didn't try to tag along as much. I stayed close to my sponsor and when necessary called my friends on the Al-Anon list. I thought that my new sense of purpose and giving David the space he sought would draw us closer together.

On the contrary, my new path forged a bigger rift between us. On more than one occasion, David expressed hurt feelings because I had opened my heart to strangers and taken their counsel. He felt that I was giving them credit for things he had tried to point out to me for a long time. I tried to assure him that I heard his complaints and that they were one of the main reasons I sought help. He didn't understand that when he and others confronted me about my behavior, they acted as if I had misbehaved on purpose. None of them understood the deep-seated reasons for my behavior; they all just told me that I had to change. True, but how on earth was I supposed to do that? Someone had to show me.

Some members of my family, not understanding that my sanity hung in the balance, didn't see why I found it necessary to go to meetings and accused me of neglecting my husband

and children. Others told me that only weak people needed those kinds of places. Looking back, I can understand how unsettling it must have been for my family that I sought help outside the bounds of what was familiar. Speaking openly about issues that were affecting all our lives appeared to them to be betrayal. I think they thought that I was painting them out to be the bad guys, but in reality, the opposite was true. I was discovering the driving force behind our afflictions, and the information gave me more compassion for everyone involved.

When I started focusing on myself, I realized that my thoughts had been becoming more obsessive-compulsive. I'd worry myself sick over one pervasive thought for an entire day. I found warfare Scriptures in the Bible and prayed them ritualistically like chants. Praying the Word over our circumstances is a wonderful thing, but I was putting my faith in empty repetition, not in the Lord. If I missed one day of quoting those Scriptures, I felt guilty and certain that I'd left the door open for the devil to wipe us all out. My prayers were becoming bondage. The Lord wasn't my defender; I was.

House cleaning and maintaining order became a solace for me. The standing joke was no longer about Mama Hall; I became the focus of ridicule as I took over where she left off. Everyone knew that if they left a plate, spoon, or glass for a second, I would wash it and put away. My surroundings had to be neat, quiet, and predictable. And just like Mama Hall, I didn't like to have a lot of children playing in the house. Unbeknownst to me, I was re-creating my sterile childhood and passing on nuttiness to another generation.

By this point in my life, I understood Mama Hall's irritability and control issues and had adopted her coping mechanisms as my own. I'm just grateful that David counteracted my pathology by surrounding our kids with other children, and fun, fun, fun. I didn't know the meaning of fun. I had always been an adult, and there was no place in my head for frivolity.

I also lived with pervasive feelings of dread. I didn't understand why until the day I learned in a meeting that my uneasiness was called a "feeling of impending doom" and that such feelings are common in alcoholic homes. Anyone who has lived with alcoholism for any length of time knows how one wrong word can easily ruin a perfectly good day. Everything can be going beautifully one moment, and the next an argument or something worse can erupt without warning. This had happened frequently throughout my life, and when it did, I usually got hurt. So even when things were peaceful, I lived like a soldier with post-traumatic stress. Figuratively speaking, I was always ready to grab my M16 and fire.

That old deep sense of loneliness and need never left me. I had thought being married would fill that void, but it didn't. Marriage was never designed to fix emotional brokenness. I battled feelings of abandonment every waking moment. I felt secure and safe whenever David was around, but I knew that my insatiable need was smothering him and that I couldn't run to him any longer. To release my pent-up emotions, I ran to the Lord and went to meetings instead. I needed the help desperately, and both made me feel peaceful inside.

Sometimes I was criticized for not being as supportive as I had been before I started going to meetings. But what I was really trying to do was to take off my God-suit and focus on removing the beam from my own eye, so I wasn't as compliant as before.

Despite being accused of neglecting my family, I wasn't irresponsible. I did my share of the housework and laundry during the day before the meetings. I wasn't a slouch who was abandoning her family to hang out with other disgruntled housewives. The boys had their dinner, baths, and did their homework. I took coloring books, snacks, and little games to occupy them during the meetings, and they got to play with other children whose parents were seeking help for their families. The meetings lasted only an hour and a half; we were back home and the boys in bed by nine-thirty.

There was a remarkable emotional change in the boys when I started attending meetings. They were also more peaceful. I was providing stability, structure, and a routine for them. They were interacting with familiar faces, and they no longer had to worry about me waking them up late at night so I could drive aimlessly through the city, crying like a madwoman.

The most painful criticism I experienced was being told that I was displeasing the Lord and dabbling in the occult by going to 12-step meetings. Some people were put off by the fact that Al-Anon referred to a higher power but didn't mention Jesus. *Am I being deceived into going down this path?* I often asked myself. *If the devil is behind this, why would he lead me to recovery and bring me so much hope?*

I sought the Lord tearfully because of the things that were being said against me. I had to decide whether I was going to crumble under pressure or keep going in the light of what I believed the Lord had revealed to me.

It's ironic that most of the people I came in contact with in meetings were neither unbelievers nor involved in the occult. They were "underground" Christians, saints who were hiding out, too afraid to reveal to their pastors and congregation that they were struggling with addictions and other compulsions. They had been told, just as I was, that 12-step programs were demonic.

This troubled me deeply. I often wondered, *Why are these Christians ashamed and hiding out?* Hiding from other believers, no doubt. There was something terribly wrong with that picture. For a long time I was angry with church leaders for not making themselves accessible to God's emotionally broken people. It was okay to pray for salvation, healing, financial help, backslidden loved ones, and God's direction, but in the eighties I had yet to witness believers being given the freedom to confess dark, hidden struggles in prayer circles.

Twelve-step programs don't claim to be the pathway to salvation. That's what churches, pastors, and believers are for—to guide the lost to the single most important step in their lives, finding salvation through Jesus Christ. If churches were always safe places where people could go to talk to somebody and get a hug, maybe 12-step programs wouldn't be necessary. But, sad to say, that is seldom the case. In fact, many people have been abused under the guise of God and religion. To be safe and stay clear of controversy, Al-Anon chose to use the concept of a "higher power," and I never found it a conflict of interest that we were asked not to discuss religion (or politics) in meetings.

Jesus said, "I am the way and the truth and the life. No one comes to the Father except through me" (John 14:6). While Christians embrace the truth that Christ is the only path to God, there are many paths that can lead a person to Christ, and 12-step programs can be one of them. Looking at one's character flaws, confessing sin, asking forgiveness, and depending totally on a higher power are in no way contradictory to the Bible. Even if some chose a tree as their higher power, their choice does not invalidate the principles behind the twelve steps. My higher power has always been Jesus Christ.

205

Twelve-step programs are a means to help those who are hurting—including Christians—and meetings are a place where they can share their deep pain and lend a supportive ear to one another. For me, the meetings were similar to the vision that my dear friend Jill Miller had for people centers.

I had been a Christian for more than ten years when I started recovery, and my personal relationship with the Lord improved immensely. The phrasing of the third step jumped out at me: "Make the decision to turn our will and our lives over to the care of God, *as we understand him.*" So far, my understanding of God had been based on the interpretations and opinions of others. I now realized that I was not a product of a Christian assembly line and that I had a personal relationship with the God who had created me as a unique individual.

I knew that I was a part of the body of Christ, not the

Lone Ranger, and that I had to obey God's Word. I wasn't trying to be a rebel or a nonconformist, but I was tired of feeling that I had to ask the world's permission to get well. I had to make peace with the fact that others might not agree with me about the path I had chosen. My past actions had left me vulnerable to criticism, but that was drawing to an end. My life was a private matter between the Lord and me, and what others thought of me was not my business.

Having the freedom in meetings to express my feelings and explore both the positive and negative aspects of my relationship with the Lord brought me closer to Him. I'm not suggesting that receiving Jesus in my heart as my Lord and Savior was not sufficient. Jesus is all I will ever need, and I love Him with all my heart. What I am saying is that as a result of being able to express my true feelings, I developed a stronger faith. Meetings were a place to go and work out my salvation daily with the holiest fear and trembling.

On my thirty-second birthday someone gave me *A Shepherd Looks at Psalm 23*, by Phillip Keller, and the Lord used that book to encourage me that I was on the right path. The author, a former sheepherder who eventually became a pastor, talked about how sheep are creatures of habits that can lead to their own demise. If it were left up to them, they would stay in the same spot and eat the grass until the land became a barren wasteland. Despite the fact that sheep resist change, it's a shepherd's job to constantly move them to richer pastures.

Keller also said that of all the animals created, sheep need the most care and direction. They pass disease back and forth from daily contact, and if they aren't fed and cared for properly, their digestive system can't handle a rich diet. Even if the shepherd leads them to greener pastures, abused sheep can't immediately eat the same diet as healthy sheep. They have to undergo a long period of confinement and a bland diet in order to be restored to health.

When I read that, I cried with relief, for I knew for certain the Lord was speaking to me about the condition of my life. I wanted with all my heart to move to greener pastures, but I wasn't healthy enough to achieve my goals. The Great Shepherd had to heal and restore me first. If I wanted a different life, I had to trust Him to lead me on the right path out of the old places into new territory. My job was to follow. Rejoicing in the Lord for the wonderful present of Keller's book, I set forth with renewed determination, and I never looked back or questioned my path again.

PART IV

On the Potter's Wheel

DREAM CODA

FOR MY MOTHER

I am walking on a beautiful college campus. Other women are walking beside me, holding on to me for dear life, looking for direction. Even though nothing is familiar, I find the front gates. I look around a bit confused. I have never been here before, but I notice to my surprise that there are white sturdy fences all around. The elderly, frail residents who live in this area are well protected. Their home is secure, orderly, neat, and peaceful.

I am relieved to be here, but as I look to the right and then the left, I realize that I don't know which way to go. I am frightened for a moment. All of a sudden, I look in the distance to my right and see my mother waving her arms above her head.

"Come here, Lolita," she says. "Over here. I've saved a place for you."

I walk toward her, engulfed in tears of relief and so happy to see her. As I make my way to join her, I feel that in spite of our tumultuous past, she, in her own way, has been there to make a way for me, and I love her.

Chapter Eighteen

STEPPING AHEAD

I have often heard people complain that therapy coddles people and excuses their bad behavior. Yes, any right-on form of therapy will provide comfort and understanding—but it will also confront people who are suffering and challenge them to take a closer look at their actions. Insisting that all problems are external is a telltale sign that a person has not truly surrendered to the therapeutic process. Therapy that is from the Lord exempts no one from accepting responsibility for his or her own wrongdoing and the consequences of it.

As I stepped ahead in the Al-Anon program, I learned that the twelve steps were not one-time events, but a way of life. I also found out how truly hard it is to take some of the steps. When it came time for me to take the fourth step— "make a searching and fearless inventory of ourselves"—I found it devastating to face my character defects and confess my part in my turbulent circumstances. I was afraid and vulnerable when I opened up and admitted fault.

The eighth step was also difficult: "Make a list of all persons we had harmed and became willing to make amends to them all." I was afraid to approach the people I had written on my list to ask their forgiveness. Gert told me that the amends were for me. Making them allowed me to come clean before the Lord and to begin healing my relationships.

I had already apologized to my mother for hurting her and not heeding her counsel, and on more than one occasion I reached out to Shelly to confess my deep sorrow for hurting her. Now I made amends to David as well. That was very hard to do because his family was part of my ongoing struggles, but it was a start. When I saw Ari at a family gathering, I told him that I was sorry for speaking to him in such a disrespectful manner during the divorce and thanked him for adopting me and for providing me with so many opportunities. Later, my amends broadened to family members in Chicago for my hypocrisy. As my children got older, I made amends to them as well.

To my utter surprise, I started to get calls out of the blue from men I had had relationships with. I knew those calls were no coincidence. The Lord wanted me to make restitution for my part in our immoral acts. I wrote letters to those I couldn't contact by telephone to ask their forgiveness. I felt embarrassed and ashamed while confessing my promiscuity, but I wanted to be cleansed from my past.

Nothing magical happened, and my problems didn't disappear, but humbling myself before the Lord, confessing my sins, and making amends were major steps. In most cases, people were gracious and forgiving. As I confronted and repented of my destructive lifestyle, I felt a crushing weight lift from my heart.

By this time, David was under great financial pressure. Besides providing for his daughter, the boys, and me, he was helping out various family members. He was strapped and needed my help. Though I wanted to stay at home and take care of the boys, my wishes were putting an even greater strain on our marriage, and it was evident I had to find a job.

The time had also come for me to start taking care of myself as I had done before marriage. Singing was out of the question because my children were too young for me to travel, and I didn't want to do club work anymore. I had had a few short-term office jobs since the birth of Nikolas, but nothing substantial. I had done receptionist work answering phones for a mortgage company, but I needed more skills. I decided to go to adult night school at the local high school to learn how to type.

213

To my amazement, I discovered that I wasn't as stupid as I had always thought I was. I caught on very quickly, and at times the other students even sought my help. I felt like a lost part of myself was coming back to life. I really enjoyed the class and got an A in it. From there, I contacted an employment agency. I was nervous taking the placement test for a clerical position, but I was elated when I typed thirty words a minute under stress. It was a milestone for me.

The agency sent me to L&F Industries, a manufacturing plant in Huntington Park that was looking for a receptionist with light clerical skills. The company was located in an industrial section of town, and the buildings looked like war bunkers. As I drove by them, I thought, *My life sure has taken a turn from performing for the president of the United States.*

I parked my car and waited a few moments to calm myself before I went inside. A cheerful, attractive young woman greeted me. She shook my hand and introduced herself as Eva. She said that she was transferring to the accounting department and that they were filling her position as receptionist. Eva made me feel at home, and I began to relax.

She handed me an application to fill out. I felt strange as I answered the questions. All of my previous job references were from show business. I hesitated to put down my salary for touring with Debby Boone, as the receptionist position paid just a tad above minimum wage. I feared that whoever reviewed my application would think I was either a big liar or crazy. I wasn't concerned about the wages. I wanted the *job*. I had no choice but to tell the truth, so I filled it out and sat there, waiting to be called in for an interview.

Eva paged someone. Soon a nice-looking woman came to the reception area, and Eva introduced her as Liz, the director of the accounting department. If I were hired, I would be working directly under her. She was kind, down to earth, and just as warm and gracious as Eva. Both of them liked me, but other applicants had to be interviewed and I had to meet one more person, Stan, the head of Human Resources. He would make the final decision. Stan was nice but all business. He looked over my application and asked, "Why aren't you still singing?" I told him that I was married with two small children. My answer seemed to suffice. He asked me more questions and said he would make his decision by the end of the day.

Although I was hopeful when I left, they never called. A few weeks later David told me I should contact them. "If they were interested in me, they would have called," I protested.

Nevertheless, I took his suggestion and called. Eva was glad to hear my voice, and she put me through to Liz right away.

"Can you come in tomorrow?" Liz asked.

"Are you kidding?" I asked.

"No," she said, "the girl Stan hired went to lunch and never came back."

I told her I'd be there in the morning.

I hugged David and thanked him for his suggestion.

When I showed up the next day ready for work, Liz told me that she and Eva had pushed for me to have the position, but Stan had been concerned about my show business background. He feared I'd go back on the road and leave them hanging. The girl who took the position had walked off the job because the phones were too demanding, and they hadn't been able to find anyone else to fill the position. I believe the Lord held the job for me.

215

Except perhaps for Eva, everyone hated sitting at the phones because they considered it boring. Not me; I loved it. It took me about two weeks to learn the extensions throughout the plant and the pager numbers of the sales department. After that, I was off and running. I got along well with my co-workers and interacted comfortably with the vendors and the clients that visited our plant. If all my work was done and no one needed my help in other departments, I was free to read and write in my journal. I basked in the privacy and peace, and the Lord used those quiet times to knit my throbbing insides back together.

Because we worked in an industrial neighborhood, there were a lot of men working in the area, and at first I felt self-conscious wandering around by myself. Without my asking her or revealing any of my insecurities, Liz offered to cash my paychecks when she did the company banking. She ran other errands for me during her breaks, and I could go to her with any problem.

As I took on more clerical responsibilities, I became intimidated. I had never held down a full-time office position, and the new tasks frightened me. I doubted my competence. No one would have known by my jovial demeanor at the front desk that I was constantly fighting a little voice inside that was saying, *I can't do this job.* An angel in purchasing named Jeff watched over me. I kept miscalculating the prices when I typed up purchase orders, and Jeff patiently took me aside and walked me through every step until I caught on. He never made me feel bad or stupid for not knowing.

The Lord used Liz and Jeff as nurturing support to help me through those troublesome times until I could stand on my own two feet. Over time, the company praised me for my efficiency on the telephones and my great rapport with the clients. I was told on many occasions that I was one of the best receptionists L&F had ever had. My clerical evaluations were satisfactory. I wasn't ever going to be an executive secretary, but I was holding down the fort. More importantly, I was no longer walking through life feeling numb, disoriented, or detached as before. It was as if parts of me that had been dead for the past thirty years had awakened.

There were many personal little touches of God's love and provision for me on the job that others may have deemed insignificant. Without fail, someone brought me a hot cup of coffee to start the day. Our office was inside a huge warehouse that had been converted into office spaces, and it was often cold inside. The company provided each of us with a little heater to keep by our desk, and my coworkers teased me that, rain or shine, mine was always going.

Because L&F was a machine shop, it had an account with an auto repair shop nearby that gave the company discounts on their cars and trucks. We employees could take our cars to the same mechanic and 5A our payments. This meant that a small amount of money was deducted from our paychecks until the debt was paid. Bill and Ron, two guys who worked in shipping and receiving, helped us ladies when we had car problems—and I had a lot of them! They would help us get our cars to the shop and then drive us back to work.

217

There was an elderly employee named Haden who was a wonderful cook. Every day at lunchtime he would heat up one of his masterpieces from the night before and share his meal with me. His generosity helped me through many financially lean times because I didn't have to buy lunch.

There was another special thing about my lunch hour. All the other employees had lunch at noon, but I had mine from 1:00 to 2:00, which allowed me to listen to one of my favorite Bible-teaching programs on KKLA. When I found out that KKLA was going to replace this show with a new one at 1:00, I was disappointed, but the show turned out to be *Minirth and Meier,* and it would revolutionize my life.

At first I had no idea what the program was about. The two hosts, Dr. John Townsend and Dr. Henry Cloud, had a clinical practice based solely on the Bible and the Lord's principles of restoration and healing. I soon learned that they were gifted in both pastoral counseling and clinical psychology and that their ministry combined addressing emotional disorders and comforting distraught callers and instructing them in the Word. At the time I knew of only one Christian radio personality who spoke candidly about recovery—Rich Bueller—and I caught the tail end of his show every day when I drove home from work. His vulnerability and honesty in revealing his own struggles had encouraged me to keep fighting.

After the first *Minirth and Meier* show, I lowered my head and wept. I couldn't believe what my ears were hearing. I had been going to Al-Anon for some five years by then, and I still had no idea that in-depth information like this was out there. In essence, every day God provided me with an hour of daily therapy and comfort.

I discovered that two women at the company had been attending Al-Anon for years. One of them became my prayer partner and closest friend. She and I walked daily during our breaks, interceding for each other. Since Gert had moved on, the other woman became my sponsor. She was a strong woman with a good heart, and she ministered to my brokenness on many levels.

My new sponsor confronted me about my lack of confidence and my dependency on men. She challenged me to quit expecting David to meet all my needs and to stay out of his business. She had me make a schedule of constructive things to do to occupy my time and learn something new. When I finished the list, she congratulated me. "Good," she said. "Now live by it, and let your husband breathe." One of the results of refocusing my attention was that I began writing songs again, a desire I had lost a long time ago.

Eventually, I had to stand on my own two feet. When Liz and Jeff left the company, the pain was as excruciating as it had been when I left Chicago as a child. I didn't understand the intensity of my feelings. As nice to me as they were, I hadn't known them long enough to account for the despair I felt. I had grown too attached to them, and I knew deep inside that this change was imperative for my growth.

219

I established close relationships with other men and women at work and started sharing the Lord with some of them. A woman named Lorraine took Liz's place. She spent her lunch hour sitting in a chair near my desk eating and doing needlepoint. She was a good listener. Through her influence I began to take notice of the world around me. Before, I had been too preoccupied with the personal trauma of survival to read newspapers or keep up with politics. David was interested in talk radio programs, and he wrote rebuttals to the newspaper articles he read, but I had no such interests or convictions. I had never felt a part of any community, and I didn't believe my opinion mattered one way or another.

Lorraine loved politics, and she was up on all the current affairs. She'd ask me questions like, "What do you think about government spending?" I'd just stare at her as if she were from another planet. Who cared? But after months of listening to her, I began to listen to talk radio and read the paper, and I slowly became more interested in what was going on around me. Without realizing what was happening, I began to formulate my own opinions. My world was broadening, and I was establishing an identity.

I had a rich network of girlfriends from work. I visited their homes, our children played together, and we went to movies and birthday parties. One of them, Beverly, had two sons the same ages as my boys. We spent many potentially lonely weekends together seeking the Lord for direction in both of our lives. She and Lorraine were like sisters to me. They listened to the *Minirth and Meier* show on the radio, too.

Dr. Townsend and Dr. Cloud also had a program called Monday Night Solutions every Monday night at seven-thirty in the Radisson Hotel. It was a lecture with questions and answers at the end, and one day Bev suggested that the three of us go see them in person in Irvine. We began attending regularly, and Monday Night Solutions became an integral part of my routine for the nine years I worked at L&F Industries.

Chapter Nineteen

THE CHILD WITHIN

When I began attending Monday Night Solutions, I thought about my earlier pleas to the Lord that He fill me emotionally, as He had done for the Woman at the Well. This lecture series was one of the things the Lord used to repair the crack in my cistern so it could hold the living water He had promised.

Monday Night Solutions opened up a whole new stratosphere of education for me and gave me insights into the emotional issues challenging the Christian community. I became aware of the severe impact early developmental injuries can have on adults, and I became familiar with terms like *boundaries, enmeshment, bonding, resolving good and bad splits,* and *character and attachment disorders.* At last I had names for all the dysfunctional behaviors I had been enmeshed in since childhood.

I had never before heard counsel that supported being average. I had struggled my entire life to be the ideal person.

Now I found freedom in embracing the fact that there was no such thing as a perfect person. I was truly on the road toward healing when I came to terms with the reality that I was a creature, not the Creator.

Townsend and Cloud often spoke about the importance of being in a community where people really knew all aspects of you, the good as well as the bad. I went to meetings, but I still didn't let people know when I was struggling, and I still felt shame whenever I made mistakes. But the doctors' message was that until you reached out and brought safe people into your dark places, you'd continue to live a depressed, isolated life.

My personal life was falling apart, and my marriage was at death's door. My anger, bitterness, and resentment were at all-time high, and I cried a lot. It was hard working full time, grieving my failed marriage, and trying to hold myself together for the sake of my sons at the same time as I was facing the demons of my past. I needed extra emotional support to help me through those painful times. Having a paycheck gave me the opportunity to see a personal therapist, so I decided to take the next step *Getting Them Sober* suggested. One day at one of the Monday Night Solutions meetings, I asked if anyone knew of a good therapist. After the meeting a woman handed me a card. The name on it was Gordon Broderson. A few weeks later I summoned the courage to call and make an appointment.

Gordon's office was in a small church in a quaint, peaceful neighborhood twenty minutes from my home. It was a smoldering hot day. Luckily, I had an evening appointment, and it was cooler when I walked inside the church. There weren't a lot of people around, and it was very quiet. I sat in the waiting room listening to the soothing instrumental music playing overhead while my boys played quietly at my feet with their toy cars. Not long afterward a soft-spoken, nice-looking older gentleman of medium height walked out of the office.

"Lolita?" he asked.

"Yes," I said. I rose to me feet and stepped toward him.

He extended his hand and shook mine. "Hello, I'm Gordon," he said. "Please come on in." He showed me a room next door where the boys could play during my session.

I pretty much knew what my problems were at the time, but I didn't know what to expect in therapy. I had come to grips with the alcohol issues in my family and had attended meetings on sexual abuse. I thought individual counseling would sew up the remaining loose ends, and I planned to see Gordon for only a few months. I figured he'd give me some pat answers and send me merrily on my way.

There was a gentleness and fatherly kindness about Gordon, and I felt comfortable right from the start. He sought my permission before starting our sessions with prayer. I was delighted to find out he was a Christian. I needed that spiritual foundation to feel safe.

"Tell me about yourself," he said.

I started by talking about my marital problems, and it was a while before we started tackling my past. However, I noticed that whenever Gordon asked me how I felt about anything, I went numb. My feelings seemed to seep out through my pores. It troubled me that I couldn't access my emotions. They were buried deep beneath the surface, and I didn't know how to release them. I was a master at giving people the answers I thought they wanted to hear, but now I couldn't manufacture the results Gordon sought. Not being able to pretend any longer was one of the first clues that therapy wasn't going to be an easy process.

My early sessions dealt with my concerns about being a better wife and mother. I made sure that I told Gordon about my character defects. I showed him my inventories and the amends I had made. I wanted to please him and let him know that I was serious about getting well. Gordon listened intently and didn't say much. One day, however, he took me off guard.

"You've certainly done a lot of good work," he said. "You've made amends to all but one person."

His remark puzzled me. I couldn't think of anyone I had left out. I expected him to chastise me for not working my program correctly.

"Who did I miss?" I asked.

"You!" he said. "You have painstakingly taken care of everyone else's feelings. Now we have to find yours." That surprised me. I had never considered making amends to myself.

Gordon drew a small circle on the chalkboard and a big circle around it. He put my name in the middle of the little circle, and entitled it OHC (the original hurting child). In the larger circle around my name he wrote in the word *defenses* (the false self). Pointing to the board, he showed me how the two related to each other. He said that I had developed coping skills to mask my true feelings and used them as a shield to protect myself. He named the various tactics people use to deny the pain of childhood.

Codependency led the pack. Addiction to work, food, drugs, anger, alcohol, gambling or sex, overspending, rage, and depression were just a few of the other things he wrote down. I recognized practically everyone I knew somewhere on that list.

"We have to get through your defenses to find the real you," Gordon said.

He explained that I felt much safer being numb than allowing myself to feel the intensity of my emotions. He kept referring to the little girl inside and how she was all alone, fending for herself emotionally. I had never viewed myself as a needy, defenseless child. Throughout my life I had been praised for being mature for my age. It was unsettling to hear that my maturity may not have been an asset.

I couldn't grasp what Gordon was saying. To help me understand, he gave me an assignment for the following week. He told me to look around at a market or a park for a little girl around the age I was just before I left Chicago. "When you find her," he said, "imagine her with the same responsibilities and challenges you faced at her age."

I thought it was a strange assignment, but I agreed to do it. One day while I was walking back to my car after dropping Joseph off at school, two little girls came out of one of the classrooms. One of them was carrying an envelope, and together the girls headed for the office. They couldn't have been more than six or seven.

The little girl carrying the envelope caught my attention. She was so tiny and delicate. Even though the distance from the classroom to the office was only a few feet, the teacher had the presence of mind not to send the girl alone. I did

225

what Gordon asked me to do and envisioned myself at her age. I cringed thinking about that child facing some of the challenges I had.

I sat silently in my car for a long time. I could feel sad about that little girl being abused and neglected, but I still felt detached from my own experience. However, I understood more of what Gordon had wanted me to see. I had never seen myself as delicate, innocent, and incapable of fending for myself. I wasn't pure like those little girls. I had always seen myself as an adult who could handle anything that crossed my path, and in most cases I had. It never occurred to me that I was still only a child. After that experience at Joseph's school, I began to slowly emerge from denial.

226

Gordon helped me to silence the voice in my head accusing me of attending too many meetings. With just one sentence, he set my heart free. "A mom who goes to meetings is much healthier than a suicidal one," he said.

I hadn't realized that my thought processes had become dangerous. I hadn't actually thought about taking my life since I was sixteen, but I had to admit that my preoccupation with making a will was strange. I was always worrying about who would take care of my boys.

"Where will *you* be?" Gordon asked me.

I didn't have an answer. We discussed the possibility of putting me in treatment for a few weeks, but I didn't want to leave my boys that long. So Gordon saw me at least twice a week and put me in a women's support group immediately. There were times when I came to my sessions depressed and unable to speak. I remember once just staring hopelessly out the window while Gordon sat by quietly.

As the months passed, vivid dreams became an every night occurrence. I was taken aback by the frequency and intensity of them. My sessions were dealing with my present life, but to my dismay, my dreams were about JB. How could that be? All that had happened years ago. I never thought about JB. Obviously, he was a wound I had pushed way to the bottom of my soul. The Holy Spirit began His work. For six months I cried in my dreams as I confronted JB with how awful he had treated me. Finally, the dreams stopped. I found it hard to believe that I had harbored all that resentment without knowing it.

After the JB dreams, I started dreaming about my childhood in Chicago and my grandparents and the Halls. I dreamed that a stranger hidden from view was trying to apprehend me. Dreams about my childhood lasted the entire time I was in therapy—more than fifteen years.

I kept a pink notebook filled with the dates I received personal Scriptures and prophetic and therapeutic dreams during the long, tedious journey toward healing. I have stacks of journals I've kept over the years. I kept them because I wanted to remind myself that getting over childhood trauma is painfully hard work, not effortless as some Christians suggest.

One day I told Gordon about an incident in my childhood and a conversation I had had with one of my cousins on a visit to Chicago when I was fifteen.

One day when I was a child, my neighbor and I were

waiting for one of my cousins to come out and play. "Say," he asked, "how come you look so much like your cousin Julie?"

"What are you talking about, boy?" I asked. "I'm supposed to look like her; she's my cousin."

"Nuh-uh," he said. "You don't look like all of your cousins. You look exactly like Julie. You look more like her sister than her cousin."

He forgot the conversation, but I didn't. Others had pointed out the similarity between my Hansen cousins and me. Julie was one of my aunt and uncle's four daughters. I was two years older than her, and she and I played together all the time. I was proud to look like her. It was proof that I belonged in our family. Not having sisters of my own, looking like Julie was the next best thing. However, my neighbor's question made me uneasy.

Outsiders were making the same observation, and at times they would point their fingers and whisper when I came in the room. As soon as I got close, the whispering stopped. I pretended not to notice, but I felt self-conscious and ashamed by the scrutiny because by then my Uncle Hansen was sexually molesting me. However, I shoved my feelings deep down inside and said nothing.

When I was fifteen, all the feelings came surging back in a conversation with one of my cousins.

"You should know this," she said. Aunt May told me that your father isn't dead. I know who he is."

My mouth went dry, and my heart raced in my chest. I was afraid to say anything, but I eventually had to. "Who is it?" I asked.

228

"Uncle Hansen," she said. My eyes must have widened in horror.

"What are you saying? That can't be true."

"I got it from a pretty good source," she said. "Aunt May would know. Go ask her. She thinks it's awful that no one ever told you the truth."

I didn't answer her, but my mind was swirling. *My uncle? The man who sexually molested me when I was little? It can't be.*

Later on that evening, I tearfully told Mama Hall what my cousin had told me. She kept washing the dishes. "I don't know anything about that," she said. "I'm not the one to ask."

I figured that if Mama hadn't heard it, it couldn't possibly be true. She would have known something that awful. I didn't want it to be true, and I had no intention of asking my mother that terrible question or of ever bringing up the subject again. I buried the information down deep inside and never discussed the situation again.

229

After I told Gordon the story, he said, "You need to find out the truth about your uncle." He said it was time to go back to Chicago and find out.

Before my trip, I dreamed of a sympathetic judge dressed in a black robe who showed me some coffins. He had tears in his eyes as he said to me, "I'm sorry, but it's time."

Chapter Twenty

THE CRAZINESS STOPS HERE

ad Hall was sick with emphysema, and he passed away a few days after I arrived. A few weeks later Mama Hall died from complications of diabetes. The only consolation I had was that several years earlier, both Mama and Dad had rededicated their lives to Christ. It was comforting knowing that they were together in the arms of Jesus, but losing both of them so suddenly left me shaken.

Not long after their deaths, I became involved in an ugly lawsuit. Dad Hall had befriended a family for many years. They weren't blood relatives, but he loved them as family and considered their two daughters his nieces. Unbeknownst to Dad, one of those lovely nieces was a barracuda, and in the midst of my sorrow at losing both my parents, I had to hire an attorney to fight for the inheritance they left me. The whole experience was a devastating crash course in resisting evil. Even though I was under severe attack, God was strengthening my faith to trust Him, for rougher weather lay ahead during my stay in Chicago.

While my legal affairs were being settled, I went to see my Uncle Hansen. His oldest daughter went with me. She needed answers, too.

My uncle had gained quite a bit of weight. He wasn't the handsome, powerful figure who had once loomed in the background of my young life. Life had beaten him down. He acted as if he had been expecting a visit from me. The three of us sat down at the kitchen table and made small talk for a time. Eventually, the conversation shifted, and I told him I needed closure and to have it, I had to confront the rumors that had swirled around my life.

"Are you my father?" I asked point-blank.

He looked at his daughter, then down at his hands before answering me. "Yes, I am," he said.

My cousin and I looked at each other, stunned. In a split second two cousins had become sisters. Holding back my tears, my mind flashed to Chief. It was no wonder we had such a close bond while we were growing up. He was my brother.

As a child, I had longed for my father, while he had been right there all along. I remembered the family reunion pictures. He proudly took photographs with his wife and children, while my mother and I sat alone for ours. How could everyone pretend that his sickness had not mortally wounded my mother and her sister? Our families had interacted as if nothing out of the ordinary was taking place.

My father saw me take my first steps, lose my baby teeth,

and grow before his very eyes, yet he never reached out to me. His children bore his last name, but not me. I know they were not spared agony and pain in their lives from having him as a father, but at least they knew who they were and where they belonged and had one another for support. The worst thing of all was that my own father was my abuser.

I just sat there looking at him. My father had no idea how he had damaged my life. Earlier he had complimented me on my singing and accomplishments. He saw a successful singer sitting there. He had no clue how much I loathed and detested myself because of what he had done to me. I wanted to ask him, "Do you know that I can't trust men because of you? That I'm unhappy and in pain practically every day of my life because of you?" I felt sick to my stomach.

233

"How could you sleep with your wife's baby sister?" my sister asked him.

I stared at the floor in disbelief as he told his side of the story. He told us that he loved my mother, but that she was so young that Grandmother forbade him to see her. He pursued her anyway. I thought about my mother and what a weight she must have carried. I now had a clearer perspective on her pain and why she was such a troubled soul. I understood her distance now. She couldn't discuss what had happened to her.

As my father continued to talk, I knew one thing for sure. The craziness wasn't going any further. All the secrets and whispering were finally going to stop. My mind raced as I thought about everyone this revelation was going to affect. What would my brothers and sons think? My heart went out to my mother and her sister. No matter what they had both endured, my aunt never made me feel unwanted or unloved. She raised me right alongside her children.

My father said to me, "I wanted to claim you, but your grandmother wouldn't let me. I've always been proud of you."

I said nothing. I couldn't hear any more, and I left the kitchen. *You sure have a despicable way of showing love,* I thought. I felt chaotic and disoriented. All I wanted was to go back home to Los Angeles.

Before I left Chicago, I wrote my father a letter. In it I told him that I forgave him for what he had done. I wasn't excusing him; I just did not want to be bound by his sickness any longer. I told him that he must have been miserable inside to make the sick choices he made throughout his life. I spelled out the plan of salvation and pleaded with him to accept Jesus as his Lord and Savior. I told him I was in therapy and struggling to put the pieces of my life together.

I'm glad I listened to Gordon and went back to Chicago because I would never see my father/uncle alive again. He died a few years later. My oldest sister told me later that he died with my letter neatly folded in his wallet. "He must have carried it everywhere he went," she said. His children—my siblings—put my letter in the top pocket of his funeral clothes and buried it with him. I prayed earnestly that he had accepted Christ before he died. If so, God brought good out of all this tragedy.

That night as my sister and I drove away, we assured each other that even though what had just taken place was painful, it was best to finally know the truth. I didn't feel better immediately, but confronting my father marked a turning point in my life.

When I returned home, I called my brothers, Sam and Tufa, and shared the truth of my identity with them. They were quiet for a while, but both reassured me that those particular circumstances had no bearing at all on our love and relationship. My mother and I discussed the situation, but it was still a painful subject for her. All she said was that my father's version of what took place was a lie. He had told me that he loved my mother, but that she was too young. My mother said that he had never loved anyone.

By taking steps to deal with what had taken place, I put a stake in the heart of our dark, hidden family secret. Once and for all, I wanted to shut the mouth of the enemy, the accuser, and prevent him from any longer using the information as a club, especially over my mother and me.

235

Meanwhile, David and I drifted further and further apart. Eventually, after much prayer and many tears, I moved out. I felt that in order for the chaos to cease in our marriage, we both had to be going in the same direction. Since he wasn't open to counseling, we agreed to separate, and we did it in peace. In fact, the day I moved out we stood in the kitchen holding each other tight while I cried in his arms. I told him how much I loved him and that I didn't want to go but that we had to get help.

I found a cute little back house not far away from David and moved in with our sons. David kept close to the boys and provided for their welfare. He never allowed what was going on between us to keep him from spending time with his children. For the first six months I was on my own, I couldn't watch television. Everything reminded me of David. I could only listen to gospel radio and only to sermons, not music.

Unshackled was by far my favorite broadcast. The true-life dramatizations of people's testimonies encouraged me through many a storm. Late one evening while I was listening to the radio, I heard a sermon about walking with the Lord through solitary places. The speaker admonished listeners not to fear the desert, for the Lord would make His will known in those places and would instruct and guide. I would be in a desert place for a long time to come. The crushing, bruising, and planting process of Isaiah 28:23–29 was just now beginning.

On the weekends that the boys stayed with their father, our little house became more of a convalescent home. I would have nightmares about roaming the streets of Chicago between the homes of my grandparents and the Halls. The next day, I'd try to distract myself by watching old westerns on cable, but I'd end up crying the entire day. On Sunday, I'd struggle to pull myself together to attend a church service. I was still hopping between three different congregations. On Monday morning, it would be back to work making a living, balancing finances, and running a household. Many a day I looked at my children and asked myself, *I wonder how they'd feel if they knew that their mother is emotionally younger than both of them combined?* I had pushed the "little" part of myself away for years; now she was emerging, and I was frightened of her.

Gordon had spoken about the child inside, but I thought he was speaking theoretically. He wasn't. I felt little, afraid to tackle the world on my own. I battled my thoughts, which were like those of a small, abandoned child. I had been depending on

David and my mother and had no idea how to live on my own and take care of the boys. It was good that the Lord was right there to comfort me. I had another dream about Him. Jesus came to me as a high priest, but I didn't recognize Him at first. He told me not to fear, that I was in the palm of His hand. I awoke refreshed and feeling more confident.

I was still praying that David would also seek counseling and that we could eventually put our family back together under healthier circumstances. David, however, wasn't sold on the idea and wasn't convinced that we could work out our difficulties. For more than eight years I stayed in the agony of limbo. We'd spend time together for a while, but then the same personality differences that tore us apart in the first place would surface and clash once again. It was always the same merry-go-around. I wanted to be close; he wanted space. David got help for himself and stopped drinking, but our marriage was at a standstill. There were long periods of time when the only contact we had was to discuss something concerning the boys.

237

During one of those times in 1990, I had a powerful dream. I was in a doctor's office, and he told me that I was six weeks pregnant. He pointed to the monitor, "See?" he said. "It's a boy!"

You can't tell that early what the sex of a baby is, I thought. I knew that David was the father, and I was told to name the baby Seth. I asked if I would ever have a daughter. The Lord told me that He had already given me one; I was to cherish and pray for David and Shelly's daughter.

I was taken aback by the dream because I wasn't pregnant. David and I were barely on speaking terms, much less romantically involved. *Having Seth would be a miracle under the present circumstances,* I thought. I felt depressed after having the dream because David and I weren't together anymore. I thought that I was going crazy. *Why do I dream these fairy tales at night?* I wondered. Nevertheless, I recorded my dream and looked up the meaning of Seth. It means "appointed."

These dreams at times were taxing. I was upset because all of my outer circumstances were just the opposite of what I was dreaming. I had been told that the only way you knew that a message was from the Lord was by its accuracy. Thus far, many of my dreams had come to pass, but others hadn't. I used to wonder how the saints in the Bible could hear personally from the Lord and yet under pressure still doubt what they had been told. After a while I understood all too well. You feel ridiculous claiming outcomes that are humanly impossible while people look at you as if you have two heads. And yet you know that you didn't make it up or eat pizza before you went to sleep.

"Well, maybe you're dreaming things you want to happen," some people said.

That was a reasonable observation, so I told myself they were probably right. I finally got to the point where I told the Lord, "If my dreams are from You, You will have to bring them to pass. I lay them at Your altar."

After eight years, I felt that, dreams notwithstanding, either David or I had to make a move. I worked hard not to involve myself in his personal life any longer. It was clear that he didn't want to reconcile, and I finally stepped out and filed for a divorce. This was devastating to me because I wanted my family back together, but I couldn't do it alone.

I began thinking that others might be right. My dreams were just that, my dreams, and not from Lord. I listened to the counsel of people who presented themselves as more spiritual than me. "Pray for a new mate who is walking the same path as you," they said. "Start over." That made perfect sense to me, so I contacted a divorce attorney and began making plans for a new life. I wanted to start singing again and meet someone new.

But I wasn't in control; God was. After the six-month waiting period, I called my attorney because I hadn't received any documents telling me that the divorce decree was final. He told me that my paperwork had been lost. It didn't resurface until three years later, and by then any hope I had for a new relationship had vanished. The Lord wouldn't permit me to date other men. The minute I found someone I could give my heart to, he'd either move away or suddenly meet his soul mate.

239

Back in limbo again (with egg on my face) and waiting on the outcome of my wayward divorce, I decided to find a support group as Townsend and Cloud had suggested at Monday Night Solutions.

My few months of seeing Gordon had stretched into seven years, and we both knew our time together was drawing to a close. When I remember Gordon, I think of him as a father who supported me through the infancy stages of healing. I don't believe I would have allowed myself to become vulnerable if he hadn't been such a quiet, gentle man.

Now I figured I would need a divorce recovery group to help me adjust when the divorce was final, so I contacted Minirth and Meier Clinic and asked for a referral. "We don't have a divorce recovery group," their receptionist said, "but Dr. Keith Douds has a women's support group in your area."

My first thought was, *You've got to be kidding! I ain't entering no more women's groups. I'm done with in-depth therapy.* I figured I had dug deeply enough into my past. I decided that I was just about healed and that it was time for some happiness and excitement. I wanted with all my heart to be reconciled with David, but if that wasn't possible, it was time to recover from the divorce and meet someone new.

The young woman waited for my response. For some odd reason, I opened my big mouth and said, "Okay!" All the while I was taking down the information, a little voice inside was screaming, *Are you nuts? Why are we going there? We don't need any more groups!*

Chapter Twenty-One

DREAM WORK

A week later I was sitting in Dr. Keith Douds' office. He wasn't what I had expected. He was considerably younger than Gordon, and I just didn't know how to relate to a male therapist close to my age without flirting. I didn't feel flirtatious, but in my past I had taken refuge in seduction when I felt insecure, and I didn't know how to act any other way with attractive men.

Keith was pleasant and kind, but professional. I wanted to present myself as a lady. My mind was galloping as I tried to think of the right thing to say. I was a little girl staring into this stranger's piercing dark brown eyes, terrified I'd say something stupid. It was as though Dr. Douds were peering right through my soul.

I hadn't been in his office long, but I sensed that he had insight, and I felt squeamish. He wasn't relying on what I was saying, but more on what I wasn't. I projected cool, controlled self-assurance, and I began rattling on about how any moment

God was going to open the big doors for me to go sing and minister, so I wasn't sure how long I'd be around. Listening intently, Keith asked me questions. I answered them the best I could, but he made me nervous.

Keith asked me what I was looking for in therapy. I told him that I needed a group to help me emotionally adjust to my pending divorce. "I have a spot open in my Thursday night group," he said. "We discuss all types of issues." When he reminded me that it was a women's group, I told him that to be perfectly honest, I was tired of being around a bunch of women and that it was time for something new.

Keith smiled. "Okay," he said. "Why don't you give the group four weeks and then make your decision?"

"All right," I said. *It couldn't hurt,* I thought.

At Gordon's prompting, I had been in a woman's group for three months, but the female therapist never challenged the truthfulness of what I said. I could hide very well in that setting, but hiding would prove impossible in my new group. Keith Douds was patient and soft-spoken, but a master at probing and getting to the heart of the truth. Had I known that he was so proficient at smelling rats, I would have never signed up.

The day I walked into Dr. Doud's office was the beginning of a long process of untangling the web I had lived in for so long. I ended up spending years in that Thursday night support group. Keith became my therapist, friend, bear trapper, and lion tamer, and I found sisters and a deep abiding sense of love and security, though not without a price. The experience would demand much more of me emotionally than I could ever have imagined.

I pranced into my first group like an old-timer, confident of my knowledge of recovery because I had faithfully attended Al-Anon meetings and had had seven years of therapy. I didn't think I was better than the other five women in the group; I just felt I could show them a thing or two. I was determined to go there and put my good foot forward. I had no clue that my display of perfection was as glaring as a red flag to a bull. This group wasn't about being all together and not needing others.

After the first meeting, I found myself not looking forward to going back. I had never felt that way in any other recovery settings. When Gordon had first asked me questions, I felt numb, but never angry. When Keith asked me questions, I felt anger toward him. He was pushing many off-limits buttons, and I didn't appreciate it.

Keith was unyielding when faced with bull. No matter how slick you thought your game was, he let you know that he wasn't buying your act. He gave my polished act a name. He called me "Showgirl." At the time (to quote Popeye) "them were fightin' words"—even though Keith was right.

My life resembled one of the sets at Universal Studios. When you take one of those tours, you go down make-believe streets through immaculate, well-groomed neighborhoods. You see green, manicured lawns and white, yellow, and pink flowers nestled in flower beds beneath picture-perfect windows. On the outside, the houses look perfect, but when you turn the corner, there's nothing there. The homes are made of cardboard propped up by wooden beams.

Keith informed me that he was glad I had done so much

emotional repair in the past, but that he wasn't giving out Ms. Recovery awards. His goal was to meet the sad little person I really was, not the happy-go-lucky woman parading around in group. To his credit, he was confident enough to say he was sorry whenever he said things in a biting manner, and that paved the way for my feeling safe in the group. People usually didn't tell me they were sorry when they hurt me; in the past it had been my role to do the apologizing.

Still, there were times when I got up out of my seat furious, marched out the door, and slammed it behind me. I'd stand outside cussing, fussing, and kicking at the dirt. *The nerve of him,* I'd think. *Who does he think he is? He doesn't know one thing about me!* My immature parts were raging.

244

Eventually I would calm down and tiptoe back inside the room, pulling my baseball cap down to cover my face. Some of the other girls in the group were veterans and took my outbursts in stride. They already knew the ropes and had themselves been in the hot seat, as we called it. They understood what Keith was doing.

Keith often challenged me whenever I skirted the issues. "I didn't ask you what you thought," he would say. "I asked you how you felt."

I'd get angry with him, and then later we'd discuss the incident. That was the first time in my life that expressing anger wasn't a death sentence to a relationship. Throughout my life, others were permitted to be angry, even full of rage, but I had to swallow my anger and stay out of the line of fire. So to me, it was the deepest insult when the group suggested that I was angry. Keith could tolerate my anger and not abandon me because we had a disagreement

The Lord was teaching me through group that healthy people had disagreements and got angry, but that it was possible to still love a person and stay connected at the same time. I would have a hard time with that concept for a long time.

I didn't understand back then that my fellow group members were reading my body language. They paid attention to my crossed arms and my refusal to make eye contact. I often smiled and tried to act friendly when I felt otherwise, but the other women weren't buying it.

"You're smiling, but I think you're extremely angry," Keith would say.

"I am not an angry person!" I would yell. I would raise my voice and start shaking uncontrollably. I couldn't look at anyone in the room when I was in that state, so I would yell at the wall, "I am a loving, misunderstood person!" Only God knows what else spewed from my mouth. My thoughts became jumbled and chaotic, and I had no idea what I was saying.

Everyone sat patiently while my volcano erupted. When I got like that, no one in the room could touch me, look at me, or come anywhere near me. I didn't know what was happening, and once I got started I couldn't stop. Keith had the daunting task of standing on the sidelines and slowly reeling me back into the session. It was almost like trying to put a rope around a wild bucking horse. I was appalled whenever this happened. Showing anger to me was bad, a rotten testimony to the fact that I was not really a Christian. I wasn't convinced for a long time that I was an angry person. The Lord, however, began to show me otherwise by revealing the deep wounds in my character. He did this through my dreams.

At that point my dreams changed radically. I dreamed so much that people wondered if I ever got any rest. I was no longer wandering through the streets of Chicago. One of my first dreams was of a small kitten running from pursuers. The kitten finally ran into a dead end, and there was no place left to run. All of a sudden the adorable little kitty turned into a huge, ferocious lion with sharp fangs and tremendous paws with long claws. Its assailants backed up and ran.

How interesting, I thought when I woke up. I told the group the dream the following week.

Keith listened and then commented, "The kitten and the lion are both you."

He explained that the lion represented my anger. That was hard to hear. It was frightening to see how fast that soft, terrified little creature turned into a beast. Even more devastating was the fact that the dream revealed that my moods must have been escalating with the speed of light as I interacted with my family members. Keith reassured me that a sexually violated and abused woman needed a protective lion, but one that could be controlled. I felt better hearing that but also overwhelmed by the complexity of my personality.

Another time I dreamed that my car was in the parking lot at work. One of my coworkers looked out the window and saw smoke pouring out from beneath the hood, even though the car wasn't running. Everyone ran outside to see what was wrong. I didn't want anyone to open the hood and take a look. The steam was obviously the hidden rage I didn't want anyone to see.

I also dreamed about trying to hide parts of my life that were a mess. In more than one dream, I saw people from my group showing up at my front door early in the morning. I had to have things neat and in order, and nothing would be more devastating to me than to have unexpected guests. In my dream I was trying to force hats on my head to cover my uncombed hair and stuffing garbage and other items anywhere I could so no one would see the state I was truly in. No one in my dreams ever condemned me when they found me unprepared; they lived in reality. No one has a perfect home the first thing in the morning. I was my own worst judge and accuser.

247

I also dreamed that my blinds were up late at night and the lights were on, which meant that strangers driving by could look inside. I dreamed I was hiding in a closet, trying to put on makeup in the dark. I still tried to pretend that I had it all together, but it was all too clear to the group that I was a mess, and they addressed these hiding issues.

I thought about how early my need to hide had begun. My behavior went as far back to the time when I hid my poor grades from my parents and never asked teachers or anyone else for help so I wouldn't appear to be stupid. I was repeating the same patterns as an adult. I was still hiding my fear, my loneliness, my need for comfort. I pretended my shattered places didn't exist, but the Holy Spirit revealed otherwise.

God dealt with the misplaced anger and the hiding, and then the focus of my dreams shifted to abandonment. For a long time I dreamed that I was wandering through downtown back alleys, homeless. My friends were transients. I was dirty and hungry and eating out of dumpsters. I saw myself in some dreams as a mangy dog. In one dream I saw an abused Great Dane that had been horribly beaten. I knew the dog was female. She held her head down and had her tail tucked between her legs. People were throwing cans and rocks at her. Watching her, I asked myself, *Doesn't she know how beautiful and powerful she is? She's a Great Dane!*

In group, I cried as I came to realize that I saw myself as that mangy, beaten animal. One evening, Keith and my sisters had a cleansing ritual for me. I went outside and covered my face and hands with dirt. I chose Sue to wash off the dirt, which was symbolic of the filth I felt had covered me for most of my life. She put warm water and a washcloth in a bowl and gently washed me clean. It was a very emotional experience for all of us. The other girls couldn't believe how detestable my self-image was. They saw a beautiful woman, but I saw myself as vile, someone to run from.

My dreams revealed that I was searching for an identity. I would show up for work in a machine shop dressed in a beaded gown or stand out in a rainstorm wearing shorts and no shoes or hang out at a mall as a teenager trying on all kinds of clothes.

In one of my most troubling dreams, I was a younger version of myself speeding down the highway. The younger me was ignoring speed limits, changing lanes without looking around, and having a high old reckless time. The adult me was in the car behind, trying frantically to catch up and stop the other car. The younger me had no idea how reckless and dangerous she was and no regard for her own safety or the welfare of anyone else. God was showing me how I had conducted my affairs thus far. He acknowledged that I was trying with all my heart to stop myself, but I hadn't yet put the brakes on my out-of-control behavior.

Another dream summed up the complexity of my situation: I was walking through a department store, depressed, looking for a blue nightgown, but I couldn't find anything affordable. I heard an alarm go off, but I paid no attention to it because I thought it didn't have anything to do with me. A security guard took me aside and asked to see what was in my purse. I was insulted that he was insinuating I had stolen something, but I let him take a look inside. To my horror, there was the blue nightgown. I started crying and pleading with the guard for mercy. I truly didn't know I had taken the garment. The guard looked at me sternly. He believed me, but he said, "Lady, you're setting off the alarms, and you don't even know it. You'd better get some help and fast."

I was deeply troubled over that dream. Here was the woman who had entered the group considering herself already well, the same woman who had just contacted a major recording studio looking for a record deal to sing gospel music. I had all of this drama going on inside and yet honestly thought that I was healed.

Once in the course of a discussion in group, I lashed out at Keith, and on my way home later, the Lord convicted my heart regarding my actions. I promptly called Keith's office

249

and left a message apologizing for my outburst. He called back later and thanked me, saying that he understood my pain, but that my angry words had been extremely wounding. I never thought that my words had any weight or made any difference to anyone. I was dead wrong.

I dreamed that night of a huge ferocious bear roaming the woods. I knew the bear was female. She ended up at the door of a woman I didn't know. The woman's boyfriend opened the door instead. The bear opened her mouth wide, and I saw her large fangs. She bit down and mauled the man to death. The next week I shared this troubling dream in group. Keith said, "That bear is your anger. You've seen just how destructive it truly is to you and to men because of the abuse."

I had thought the dream represented something completely different, so I was disheartened by what Keith said. But deep inside I knew that he was right. Two previous dreams—the one in which I set off the store alarm and the one in which steam was seeping from under the hood of my car—were both about my unconscious rage. The dream about the bear tied everything together for me. Because of my attempts to stuff and hide my true feelings, my anger had become huge and ferocious.

My heart sank as I thought about my husband, my children, and others who had encountered my bear. I didn't know she existed, but God did. Keith's tenacity, love, and patience and the support of my sisters (who were frightened by my outbursts at times) helped me understand my anger and channel it in healthier ways. The group pointed out the benefits of having a tamed lioness, a bear, and a Great Dane as allies. What powerful animals they all were! I had always thought of myself as a weak, ineffective creature, like a snail, but my dreams said that I was much stronger than I had ever imagined. If I channeled my anger properly, I would have excellent boundaries and a means of healthy self-protection.

I had been in group for five years, and my divorce was still not final. David and I had begun spending time together again, and I was praying that the Lord would heal our marriage, but our path remained rocky. It had been ten years since the birth of Nikolas. So much time had passed that I had forgotten about having another child. To my surprise, the dream I had had five years earlier came to pass after all. On March 19, 1994, Seth David was born.

251

David was not with me during this pregnancy. He was dealing with his own chaos. My mother and family, Dr. Keith, and my sisters in group rallied and supported me during my ordeal, including the birth. In my sixth month of pregnancy, I began having premature contractions. The doctor excused me from work and confined me to total bed rest until delivery. In the midst of these circumstances, my beloved Chief, my protector and big brother, died. Just as my difficult pregnancy with Nikolas had prevented me earlier from attending Moe's funeral, I couldn't attend Chief's services because I was bedridden.

I was truly overwhelmed by his death and sick with grief. My one consolation was that Chief gave his heart to the Lord before he passed away. I knew that Chief was with Moe in heaven, and I made a solemn vow to both of them that I would do everything I could to stay in recovery and break the destructive cycle in our family.

After I had Seth and was back on my feet, I began having severe panic attacks, and that made me more determined to work even harder on my emotional baggage in therapy. My divorce came through six months later, leaving me broken-hearted over my failed marriage, even though it had been doomed from the start. I was now praying for a brighter future for David and me. I wanted God to make us both new creations in Christ.

As I continued therapy, I suffered immensely from the revelation of my festering wounds. The years during which the Lord mended me were marked by depression, despair, and confusion. The most painful revelation of all was how I viewed God and lesser authority figures.

I dreamed about uncaring, unsympathetic police officers. When I cried out for help, they came to my aid after I had already been assaulted or even murdered by an unknown assailant. Police officers stood by when my car broke down in dangerous neighborhoods, and not one of them lifted a finger to help me. Instead, they gave me a parking ticket for blocking the street.

I also dreamed of a little girl in kindergarten. She was singing "Jesus Loves the Little Children" and coloring pictures. She stopped and looked up at me with a solemn expression on her face. "Jesus helps some children," she said, "but I learned a long time ago that I had to take care of myself." She then proceeded to color vigorously.

My heart broke when I saw my strong-willed independence. I didn't know that I saw God as a punishing, neglectful police officer, but God knew all along that I didn't trust Him. That explains why I still had an awful time totally surrendering to Him. I must have felt that He had abandoned me when I needed Him the most.

I repented and asked His forgiveness. As I thought back over my life, I began to recognize that even though I had gone through a lot of anguish, God had always been right there with me, even before I knew Him. He had always protected me and made provision for my future. He had helped me and given me hope and purpose, as He had promised me so long ago through Jeremiah 29:11. Yes, I was a marred vessel, but He had me on His potter's wheel, and He was shaping me for His glory with His very own hands.

As the years passed, I grew to love and cherish group in a deeper capacity, and I took the process more seriously than ever. After a while, new problems surfaced. I started having dreams that my little girl inside was white with blond hair and blue eyes. I also dreamed of finding a baby wrapped up lying by itself, but I didn't know what gender it was. Keith felt that it was time for me to pursue individual therapy once again, but this time with a woman.

Chapter Twenty-Two

A NEW FOUNDATION

The Lord had already touched me deeply and had begun mending many of my broken parts, but I was shattered at the core of my womanhood. My natural transition from a little girl to a woman had been marred, and because of my abuse, I never had an accurate self-image. My adolescent years were also skewed by the emotional turmoil going on in my family at the time. As a result, I found being a woman appalling and shameful.

Now my task was to discover what it meant to be a healthy, godly woman. My therapists thus far had been white males, and Keith felt that it was imperative for me to meet the therapist he had in mind. God doesn't see color, and it isn't necessary to work with a therapist of the same race, but Keith and I agreed that I needed a role model who could help me embrace my identity as a black woman. He said he had just the right therapist on staff. He told me that he respected her highly and that he thought I would feel comfortable and safe with her. Her name was Cheryl Jones-Dix.

Cheryl was an attractive, stately woman with a gentle spirit and great patience, and yet she spoke candidly. At first I found it much harder to reveal my inner child to her than I had with Gordon or Keith. Before group, I had never felt comfortable with women; I had always chosen to bond with men. Therefore, for some time I carefully selected and edited whatever I shared with Cheryl. It wasn't because of anything she did; I just didn't know how she would relate to my vulnerable places. I even wore sunglasses to some of our sessions to keep from having eye contact with her.

For years, black women have been stereotyped as strong towers others can run to for comfort and guidance. We are supposed to have all the answers. The women in my own family were strong and resilient and had weathered fierce storms, sending me the message that it was cowardly to cry or show other signs of weakness. It took me a while to figure out that Cheryl was not the stereotypical black woman; she was a whole woman who struggled with life, too, but was secure enough to embrace all the aspects of her personhood, both good and bad. She helped me accept my own as I laid a new foundation for becoming the woman God wanted me to be.

Cheryl moved cautiously with me at the beginning. We didn't jump into deep waters right away. One of the first areas she began working with me on was my church hopping. She wanted to know what was behind it, and she challenged me to explore my reasons. Over time, I shared with her how much I wanted to minister in song and share my testimony with others.

"You don't have a track record for anyone to invite you to minister," she said. "Churches are careful about presenting outsiders to their congregations. You need to be rooted and planted solidly in a church home if the Lord is ever going to use you in ministry. Most congregations will want a recommendation from the pastoral staff of the church you attend, but you're conducting yourself like a stray." Her statement was an eye-opener. I had never thought about my elusiveness in those terms before, and over the next months we explored my behavior.

For some reason, one day I told Cheryl about all the people I knew who had died within a short span of time. At that point, there were fifteen in all, including Moe and Chief. Out of the blue, I told her how terrified I had been when Keith Green and his two children and John and Dee Dee Smalley and their six kids were all killed in an airplane accident. I started crying.

257

"Keith Green had a huge, successful ministry, and the Smalleys were on their way to open a new Vineyard back East. If God didn't protect them," I said, "He certainly wouldn't spare my family from tragedy."

My mistrust of God surfaced in a new light. Cheryl helped me see that I still saw God as abusive, and I discovered that I didn't want to get too close to Him or His people because whenever I got emotionally close, I got hurt. For some reason, I also felt guilty that I was still living while people I loved had died. I grieved these losses for two years.

Then in January 1996, God provided the catalyst that led me to a church home: Unexpectedly, L&F Industries laid off twenty people, including me. The following Sunday morning I decided to visit a church I had seen off the freeway in Long Beach. The name of the church was Christian Life Church.

The pastor, Don Spradling, had just returned to the pulpit from a potentially fatal illness, and his testimony of God's faithfulness ministered to me.

As Pastor Spradling spoke of how the Lord was restoring his health and faith, I felt that, like him, I was in a transition period in my life and needed a new beginning. So I decided to stick around. Even though I sat alone in the balcony for months and pretty much kept to myself, members of the congregation always greeted me with warmth and affection. I hadn't seen a large choir since I had sung in Ms. Haney's church in the fifth grade, and watching the choir in their white- and rose-colored robes and listening to them sing brought back many cherished memories.

258

Christian Life Church was the perfect setting for me to blend in, and that's exactly what I did. I made it my home. When I surrendered to the Lord by finding a church family, I began to learn more about stewardship, accountability, responsibility, service, and dependability. Best of all, I found a loving family.

I soon discovered that the pastor's wife, Kay, was the choir director. After a few months, I introduced myself to her and asked to audition for the choir. She told me that they didn't have auditions. "Just show up in the choir room on Wednesday at 7:30 PM," she said. I never said a word about having sung professionally. I wasn't looking to stand out in the church; I just wanted to find a place to fit in. I showed up and nestled quietly among the sopranos. For three years, I sang in the choir without mentioning my past.

As I did, I realized that giving us opportunities to exercise our gifts is another way God restores broken vessels. Each week as I learned the songs for the upcoming events, I felt my insides mending.

As the years passed, my sessions with Cheryl took on new dimensions. In my dreams I saw myself as a crippled woman living life in a body cast, riding in a wheelchair. I also dreamed of myself as an infant surrounded by a staff of loving doctors who were performing open-heart surgery on me. I had other dreams about injuries to the most private parts of my body. I was sore and inflamed, but a female doctor rubbed warm, soothing oil on those bruised and battered places.

There were dreams in which I beckoned to beautiful women who pampered themselves, not by indulging their vanity, but by caring for themselves. I longed to be one of them, but I felt so unworthy that I didn't know how to conduct myself in establishments dedicated to the beauty care of women.

Just because we grow up without ever getting our needs met doesn't mean those needs evaporate into thin air when we are adults. To fill the void, we need to have people in our life who support us. Our unmet needs are ever present; they just hide, and if we don't seek help, later on down the road they reemerge, often in very destructive ways.

The Lord used Cheryl to help me in these areas. My breakthroughs came when I let her touch my emotions and allowed myself to cry in her presence. I showed her that I wasn't the person in charge, as I so often projected, and I let her comfort me in those places where I still felt shame. I had never allowed other women to venture into that territory. I

259

had always taken my hurting little girl to the men in my life, only to leave them feeling trapped and overwhelmed by my need. The Lord knew my withdrawal from male dependency depended on my opening myself up to safe, loving women and allowing them access to my heart as sisters and friends. Cheryl was a safe woman I could let into my heart and lean on.

In one of our sessions, I asked Cheryl, "How would you describe your role as my therapist?"

"Well," she said, "you finally let me see your scars, and you let me walk alongside you in your pain."

As my healing progressed, I discovered a talent I had buried many years earlier. Like my grandmother, I had had a strong desire to write when I was younger, and now it resurfaced. I considered writing the only autonomous aspect of my personhood. It was a reflection of my imagination, a private place where only I could go, and a creative work of art with no fingerprints on it but my own. I love singing, but it's a very public affair. Not so with writing. I had kept a journal for years, but now a new creativity was bubbling up inside. I wanted to start writing novels.

"Isn't that just like the Lord, to reveal a hidden jewel in the midst of all your struggles?" Cheryl commented.

Suddenly I wanted to go back to school and study writing. My mother and my healing community cheered me on as I ventured into this new territory. I was afraid to go back to college after being out of school for more than twenty-five years. I knew it would be difficult, but I also knew it would be worth every minute of hard work.

I began attending Long Beach Community College. One of the prerequisites for new students was to take a career guidance course. At first I dreaded going because I would be in a class with eighteen-year-olds fresh out of high school, and I felt very self-conscious. However, God prepared the way. The teacher, Gay Gannett, was a lovely woman whose faith, exuberance for life, and honesty removed my fear about my age. She took me under her wing, and the class embraced me.

One of our assignments was to research the field we were interested in and then interview a professional in that field. I went to the English department and spoke to one of the teachers who had had his poetry published. That experience led me to take classes that would help me start a writing career. I had to learn some skills all over again, but I didn't mind. I started in the intermediate classes because I had forgotten grammar.

Every one of my instructors was a blessing. Mary Duval encouraged me to continue my journey; Dr. Velvet Pearson became both friend and writing partner. The granddaddy class for me was Frank Gasper's Novel Workshop. Dr. Pearson and I took Gasper's class together and encouraged each other through the rough spots. His class was very challenging because there were many seasoned writers in it. One good thing I had going for me was that I didn't fear criticism. I had taken the class to help me improve as a writer, not to be coddled. I wasn't, but I got a lot of positive feedback on my work and felt encouraged that I was right on track. I was proud of the fact that I took the class and faced the challenge of such steep competition.

About this time, I had a wonderful dream that reflected the handiwork of the Holy Spirit. I was my own age walking through a mall looking for something to wear for ministry. I walked out of the clothing store for teenagers, knowing I no longer belonged there. I found another store, but the clothes were for senior citizens. I asked the salesgirl for help finding clothing appropriate for my age, and she led me to a seamstress. I was about to be measured and fitted for clothes tailored specifically for me.

I thought about another dream I had recently had. At first, I was attending my father's funeral in Chicago. Later, I was an adult watching myself as a child playing in my grandparents' front yard, and the adult me began to cry. I felt the dream was speaking to me about the need for closure, and I decided to have a symbolic funeral in group.

I wrote my own obituary and chose a special song on a CD to play during the service. The group tearfully supported me as I said good-bye to the parts of my life I could never get back because of so many losses. I know this might sound strange, but the pretend funeral was the beginning of a new freedom for me. In saying good-bye to what could never be, I was saying hello to what could. In dying to how I thought my life should have turned out, I discovered that God had a much better plan.

In looking back over the course of my therapy, I'm amazed at the precision with which the Lord targeted so many wounded areas—early childhood pain, feelings of shame and hiding, abandonment, impulse disorders, fierce independence and rebellion, anger, and my inability to trust Him and authority figures. After acknowledging the brokenness my dreams revealed and working through the losses, I began feeling free inside and peaceful.

As I healed, God continued to teach and guide me through Scripture. "Plowmen have plowed my back and made their furrows long," the psalmist wrote, "but the LORD is righteous; he has cut me free from the cords of the wicked" (Psalm 129:3–4). "A bruised reed he will not break, and a smoldering wick he will not snuff out, till he leads justice to victory" (Matthew 12:20). The enemy planned from the beginning to destroy my life, but God turned what Satan meant for evil into good. There were those who spoke failure over my life, sure that I would fall flat on my face, and for a long season I had. But my smoldering wick was not snuffed out, and God came to my rescue.

263

I always tell people to never give up on loved ones no matter how grim the situation may appear or how long it has been going on. Only the Lord knows what's in someone else's heart and the beauty He can bring from the ashes of their past. We are never finished products until we enter heaven.

In time, the Lord gave me a Scripture that spoke to my heart about ministering to others: "Speak up for those who cannot speak for themselves, for the rights of all who are destitute. Speak up and judge fairly; defend the rights of the poor and needy" (Proverbs 31:8–9). I felt God impress upon my heart that people who have walked paths like my own are among the poor and needy who can't speak for themselves.

Ezekiel 34 speaks of the neglected condition of God's

sheep: they are diseased, weak, broken, and lost. In verse 4 the prophet chastises the leaders of the people: "You have not strengthened the weak or healed the sick or bound up the injured. You have not brought back the strays or searched for the lost." Many leaders in the church today do not minister to the emotionally wounded at all, and many of those who do tend to rely on pat answers and spiritual formulas that do not really help Christians seeking emotional support and healing.

The Lord mends lives in wondrous ways, but not always in the same fashion. While not losing sight of the fact that God and His Word are the foundation of all spiritual and emotional healing, we must acknowledge that we have all traveled down different paths and therefore require a different treatment for our pain. God heals, but not necessarily in ways we expect or want. God ministers individually. A diseased sheep has different needs than a broken or lost sheep. Each requires a special touch of the Master's hands.

In speaking for those who can't speak for themselves, I pray that the body of Christ will be more loving and supportive of those who find comfort in support groups and healing through therapy. And I pray that Christians will not accuse these brothers and sisters of lacking faith, of not knowing their position in Christ, or, worse, of being under the control of demons. It takes a world of faith to acknowledge brokenness and to be willing to lay open the most vulnerable places of one's life in order to become emotionally healthy.

Over the course of nineteen years, the Lord rebuilt my life brick by brick. He mended my broken cistern and filled me with peace, joy, and contentment. As the years passed, I began to dream of homes under reconstruction, freshly plowed land, and replanted gardens. God always reassured me that new, fine structures would replace the old broken-down places I had once occupied, just as He had promised me more than twenty-five years earlier. God truly gave me a new future and a new hope.

"How should I end my book?" I asked Cheryl one day. "There are so many things that are still unfolding."

Cheryl gave me a beautiful analogy. She told me that she saw me as the frame of a house. The drywall isn't all in place yet, but the floors, plumbing, and electricity are in place. You can definitely see where the rooms are going to be.

I smiled. "That would mean that my foundation to build upon is finally solid." I said.

"That sounds like a great ending to a book," she said.

I am no longer like the foolish woman of Proverbs 14 who once tore down her home with her own hands. Because God has many ways of mending broken people, I am a new creation in Christ, a worthy vessel filled with living water in the house of the Lord.

looked
ving

A WORTHY VESSEL

ne day a bunch of us sisters from group got together at a trendy restaurant in Long Beach. As I looked around the table at my sisters laughing and chatting, enjoying one another's company, scrunched together in a large booth and giggling like little girls, my heart was full.

Each woman there was courageously rewriting her own history and forging a new path out of her own struggles. I felt honored to be a part of their emotional healings, as they had been in mine. But mostly I celebrated the fact that I was truly having a great time. I wasn't disconnected and pretending to enjoy the moment, as I had done most of my life. My laughter was real. While we thumbed our noses at our diets and scarfed down chocolate cake and caramel cheesecake, I thought about where I was in life.

I now understood why my mother, who hadn't been extended much grace and tenderness as a child, had been unable to meet my needs. As the Lord continued my healing,

I came to respect her and appreciate what she had been able to give me in light of the many tragedies she herself had endured over the course of her life. Not too long ago, she and I filmed a half-hour television show called "Damascus Road." We both talked about our past and how the Lord had restored our relationship. After the program aired, I received many letters and e-mails from people around the world who were deeply touched by our testimony. My mother proudly escorts me whenever I minister, and she courageously endures as private, painful aspects of our lives are opened to public view.

My family back in Chicago can now speak candidly about the secrets that once plagued our lives. I don't have to whisper anymore or hide in shame the fact that I have half brothers and sisters and numerous nieces and nephews that I dearly love.

I enjoy holiday dinners and special times with Ari and his wife. The Lord has put a deep abiding love and gratitude in my heart for him and all that he provided in my life. He has been a very supportive grandfather.

David and I have finally found peace and are spending time together as friends. After twenty years, we can now sit across the table from each other, sip coffee, and enjoy each other's company. A couple who knew each other for six weeks before they got married has discovered that the most precious things in life can never be hurried.

God has given me back my singing. The Lord put Jay and Brenda Sterling back in my life from years ago when we both performed with Debby Boone. Jay was her bass player, and he and Brenda later started their own company. For the past ten years I have been a singer on their roster, and I perform for private parties, charities, and weddings.

God has given me a church home and an identity. I no longer felt like an alien. I have an abundance of friendships and a supportive network of recovery brothers and sisters. I have spiritual resources that sustain me in dry, lonely places during the week, and I have also begun ministering at women's functions to touch the lives of other struggling women. Joe and Nik are college graduates and, like Seth, flourishing in their own support communities.

Today, I love and trust God and His beloved Son with all my heart. There was a time when I wanted to die, but now I cherish life. And God has given me the most precious gift of all: I finally like myself.

—Lolita Robinson